CW00954391

Practical Application of Object-Oriented Techniques to Relational Databases

Practical Application of Object-Oriented Techniques to Relational Databases

Donald Keith Burleson

A Wiley–QED Publication

John Wiley & Sons, Inc.

New York • Chichester • Brisbane • Toronto • Singapore

Designations used by companies to distinguish their products are often claimed as trademarks. In all instances where John Wiley & Sons, Inc. is aware of a claim, the product names appear in initial capital or all capital letters. Readers, however, should contact the appropriate companies for more complete information regarding trademarks and registration.

Screen shots reprinted with permission from Microsoft Corporation.

This text is printed on acid-free paper.

© 1994 by John Wiley & Sons, Inc.

All rights reserved.

This publication is designed to provide accurate and authoritative information in regard to the subject matter covered. It is sold with the understanding that the publisher is not engaged in rendering legal, accounting, or other professional services. If legal advice or other expert assistance is required, the services of a competent professional person should be sought. FROM A DECLARATION OF PRINCIPLES JOINTLY ADOPTED BY A COMMITTEE OF THE AMERICAN BAR ASSOCIATION AND A COMMITTEE OF PUBLISHERS.

Reproduction or translation of any part of this work beyond that permitted by section 107 or 108 of the 1976 United States Copyright Act without the permission of the copyright owner is unlawful. Requests for permission or further information should be addressed to the Permissions Department, John Wiley & Sons, Inc.

ISBN 0 471-61225-1

Printed in the United States of America

10 9 8 7 6 5 4 3 2

To my children, Andy and Jenny,
and to Maureen, my wife and proofreader.

Contents

Preface

Because of the vast amount of academic research on object-oriented databases, it would be very simple for me to make this text highly technical and fill it with confusing jargon and mathematical equations. However, I believe that object technology is ready to depart academia and make its way into mainstream data processing. For that reason I have deliberately simplified the concepts of object-oriented database theory and created a straightforward and pragmatic book for the practicing database professional. For those interested in the theoretical background behind the concepts, I have included a complete bibliography of research on each topical area.

This book is designed to serve as a guide for the working professional or student who wishes to apply object-oriented techniques on existing database systems. Unlike many theoretical books, this book is very practical, with many examples of object-oriented techniques. Specific examples are offered throughout the text and will be presented with popular commercial databases, including dBASE®, DB2®, ORACLE®, and IDMS®.

The approach and constructs that I demonstrate allow existing "classical" databases to function within the scope of an object technology application. However, object-oriented design is not just a theory: it is the next natural evolution of database management. The next generation of databases will require that data, relationships between data, and data behaviors are all stored together and accessed in a dynamic fashion.

While the nature of object-oriented databases is inherently complex, I have tried to use simple, illustrative examples throughout the text. Some of the more complex and obscure topics such as recursive classes and multiple inheritance are also covered in separate chapters.

An Introduction to the Object-Oriented Approach

1.1.   INTRODUCTION

When object-oriented programming first became an industry fad, everyone rushed to understand this new approach to systems development. Unfortunately, many programmers perceived object technology as a new set of tools rather than as an approach to systems development. The industry has fostered this misconception with the introduction of object-oriented tools such as EIFFEL®, SmallTalk®, C++, and Versant by Object Technology®.

This misunderstanding is best illustrated with a comparison to the structured programming movement. Nicklaus Wirth, a Swiss computer researcher, introduced the PASCAL language as a remedy to the "spaghetti" code that plagued the industry. Wirth recognized that structured programming techniques dramatically reduce the maintenance of programming systems, and the PASCAL language was designed to enforce structured programming techniques. Unfortunately, many programmers mistakenly believed that structured programming could only be accomplished by using the PASCAL language.

Object-oriented systems development is a natural extension of the structured programming approach. Just as structured programming emphasized the benefits of properly nested loop structures, object-oriented development emphasizes the benefits of modular and reusable computer code, and the benefits of modeling real-world objects.

Ironically, the object technology approach started with the development of applications that could not use traditional languages such as COBOL or FORTRAN. Because object-oriented systems require careful planning, these systems were very well-defined and were very low in maintenance costs. However, it soon became apparent to the early developers that the object-oriented approach was a foreign concept for many procedural programmers. Object-oriented systems require a new way of looking at the problem.

The object-oriented languages such as C++ and SmallTalk have a very steep learning curve but, once mastered, the programmers may be many times more productive. However, the object-oriented approach is 95% philosophy and only 5% technology. Once the programmers are trained to think in object technology terms, they find that existing procedural languages may be used to accomplish many of the tasks that were once thought to be exclusively for C++ and SmallTalk. In fact, many object technology goals such as fully reentrant procedures and reusable code can be implemented with a "dinosaur" language such as COBOL. Many of the basic concepts of object-oriented programming, such as inheritance and polymorphism, can be implemented with classical languages such as FORTRAN (Meyer, 1988).

Increased productivity with object technology methods is not just a theory. Organizations that are willing to undertake the learning curve have found tremendous benefits in both reduced development efforts and lower ongoing maintenance costs (Babcock, 1993).

Many programmers of C++ and SmallTalk store their own complex objects in a file system of their own design. These "home-grown" databases are generally linked-list data structures that serve to store the objects, but they do not take advantage of the inherent benefits of a database management system. Today, many systems professionals are beginning to realize that it is possible to incorporate object-oriented functionality into existing relational database software, and some vendors are developing object-oriented "front-ends" for relational databases.

When one strips away all of the confusing acronyms and jar-

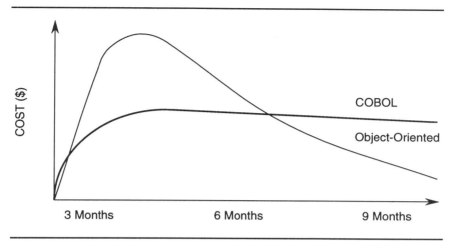

Figure 1.1. Cost as a function of time.

gon, the object technology approach is nothing more than a method, an approach to systems design that can be implemented without any changes to existing software technology.

The term "object persistence" refers to any programming technique capable of storing and retrieving the information created in an object-oriented system. Most of these "databases" are nothing more than a set of linked-list data structures that have none of the features associated with a commercial database. In the evolution of database systems, especially relational databases, there has been an emphasis of "pointerless" data storage. This means that the actual data is insulated from the user, and the user accesses his or her data with data manipulation languages such as SQL. Until recently, many major software companies have been unable to resolve the problem of incorporating relational database technology with object-oriented requirements. This book offers a solution.

Any "object-oriented" database must support the general constructs of the object technology approach including polymorphism, multiple inheritance, class hierarchies, and information hiding. Many of these features do not require a new technology; they only require modifications to the database design method. Many features of classical object-oriented programming, such as abstract data typing and multiple inheritance, are not required for most applications. Unfortunately, "object-oriented" has become a buzzword. According to Christopher Stone, the president of the Object Management Group, ". . . Sometimes it appears that every company is object oriented. How do you separate the hype from the facts? . . . For purists it should be "object orientated," but that would just confuse people further." Today, object technology is replacing object-oriented as the term to describe this approach.

The object technology method heralds the next generation of database design. Just as the first commercial databases allowed the storage of data and data relationships, object-oriented databases will store data, relationships between data, and the behavior of the data. Once data behaviors are incorporated into a database management system, these "intelligent" databases will revolutionize database systems development.

The idea of "intelligent" databases arose from the need to associate certain behaviors with certain operations on the data. The earliest attempts at this approach used Database Request Modules (DBRMs), which dynamically invoked a precompiled object module whenever a database operation was performed. For example, data record compression routines were incorporated into databases with these "triggers," which compressed the data prior to STORE or UPDATE operations and then decompressed the data items after the records were selected. The IDMS (Integrated Database Management System) database from Cullinet Corporation was one of the first database engines to have this feature.

The object-oriented approach starts with the intelligent database concept and adds additional features. Rather than being simple triggers associated with a physical event, object-oriented behaviors may contain operations that affect hundreds of database records. Also, because object-oriented behaviors are "encapsulated," no data items may be accessed or updated except through their methods. Of course, encapsulation violates the relational database concept of data independence, and any type of ad hoc data access is prohibited in the object technology model. This is a major problem with coexistence strategies for relational databases and object-oriented databases, and is fully addressed in a later chapter.

Object-oriented databases of the twenty-first century will borrow concepts from intelligent databases and enterprise modeling. An object-oriented database, unlike a relational database, requires that all relevant data entities be predefined, and corporate-wide systems of the future will require very careful data planning.

Relational databases, with their ability to join tables in an ad hoc fashion, lead many to forecast that data planning would require much less forethought, because new, independent tables are very easily incorporated into existing table structures. On the other hand, object-oriented databases demand that a complete and well-defined class hierarchy is preestablished, and that all behaviors and data attributes associated with the classes are carefully planned. The roles of the Database Administrator (DBA) and the Data Administrator, once believed to be obsolete because of the relational database, will once again become pivotal within the corporation.

After object technology has been embraced by large-scale corporate information systems, the role of the DBA will broaden in scope. Enterprise modeling emphasizes the importance of developing an overall data model, and object-oriented database systems demand a carefully planned data model.

A large corporation has thousands of objects, ten of thousands of database entities, and perhaps millions of atomic data items. A global object-oriented database for these types of companies will rely upon the expertise of the DBA to ensure that all of the class hierarchies have been properly defined.

1.2. OBJECT-ORIENTED TERMINOLOGY

Object technology is cursed with some of the most confusing acronyms known to the computer community. Nearly every month a new "OO" acronym is created, and this plethora of acronyms further obscures the approach to object-oriented methods. Chris Stone, president of the Object Management Group, states, "These terms are the 'oat bran' of software development."

For object-oriented database management, we also have a plethora of new acronyns, with new "OO" terms being introduced constantly.

MOOSE   Major Object-Oriented SQL Extensions (Melton, 1993)

FOOD   Fully Object-Oriented Database (Bradley, 1992)

OOERM   Object-Oriented Entity-Relationship Model (Gorman, 1989)

HERM   High-order Entity/Relationship Model (Thalheim, 1991)

A general list of the most common object-oriented acronyms includes:

OT   Object Technology

OOPS   Object-Oriented Programming Systems

OOA   Object-Oriented Analysis

OOD   Object-Oriented Design

OODBMS/OODB   Object-Oriented Database Management System

OOPLs   Object-Oriented Programming Languages

Many of the "OO" acronyms are losing favor. There is a trend to describe object-oriented systems as "object technology," and OT seems to be the emerging acronym to describe object-oriented systems.

There are many object-oriented societies with which you must become familiar. There is the Systems Conference on Object-Oriented Programming (**SCOOP**), the Object-Oriented Programming Systems Languages Association (**OOPSLA**), the European Conference on Object-Oriented Programming (**ECOOP**), and the Symposium on Object-Oriented Programming and Analysis (**SOOPA**).

There are many periodicals that serve the object-oriented community. These include JOOP (the *Journal of Object-Oriented Programming*), *First Class*, *Object Magazine*, and *Database Programming & Design*.

There are more then 80 commercially available object-oriented languages on the market today. Fortunately, a few of these languages have become dominant, and C++ has become the de facto object-oriented programming language, followed closely by SmallTalk. SmallTalk is favored at universities because of its "pure" object-oriented approach, and SmallTalk is becoming the PASCAL of object-oriented languages. Most students learn SmallTalk as their first object-oriented language, and later move to a more commercial language such as C++. Here is a brief list of the most popular tools and their major features.

1.3. OBJECT-ORIENTED PROGRAMMING LANGUAGES (OOPLS)

C++/Objective C®	Object-oriented extension of the popular C language
	Somewhat difficult to master
	Not pure object orientation
SmallTalk	Pure object orientation
	Syntax unlike any other language ("weird" syntax)
	Small instruction set
	Interpretive
	A good introductory language
	Does not support multiple inheritance
EIFFEL	Supports multiple inheritance
	Poor runtime performance
	Syntax similar to PASCAL
	Pure object orientation
	Very rich in functions
OOREXX®	Object-oriented extension of REXX
	Designed to work with C in IBM environments

1.4. OBJECT-ORIENTED DATABASES

The haphazard development of standards and definitions of object technology has been very confounding to most companies who are interested in using the new technology. Object technology theoreticians cannot agree on the definition of an object-oriented database, much less the salient characteristics of an object-oriented database. Many vendor products advertised as "object-oriented" capitalize on object technology buzzwords and are often very vague about the real features of the database and what makes it object-oriented. The trick for most computer managers is to separate the hype from the reality.

The "pure" object-oriented databases such as Versant® and Objectivity/DB® are very powerful tools, but they are very cumbersome to learn. Because of the complexity and the high learning curve, these types of object-oriented databases will have trouble achieving popularity in the general marketplace. A new standard for object-oriented database architecture, called the ODMG Object Model, has been proposed by a consortium of vendors, but the mega-vendors such as IBM and Microsoft have not accepted this standard.

Many object technology vendors are content to offer products that provide an object-oriented front-end to relational database engines. Others offer toolsets, which capitalize on object technology while not addressing the issue of database. A small minority of vendors offer database engines that conform to the relational database model and to object technology principles. These types of products, such as UniSQL® and OpenODB® will probably capture more market share for general database customers who are unwilling to abandon their relational database platforms.

The CORBA Architecture

Many organizations are recognizing the importance of standards in the emerging area of object-oriented systems development. In the spring of 1992 the Object Management Group (OMG), a nonprofit corporation dedicated to developing object standards, published the CORBA standard for object-oriented development. CORBA is the Common Object Request Broker Architecture, and was developed jointly by Sun, Hewlett-Packard, Digital Equipment Corp., NCR, and Hyperdesk Corporation. CORBA creates a standard protocol for an object to place requests and to receive responses from other objects. It is interesting to note that these competing vendors, who have a vested interest in proprietary software, have agreed to adhere to the CORBA standard in the development of new object-oriented systems.

1.5. THE GOALS OF OBJECT-ORIENTED PROGRAMMING

One of the primary reasons for adopting object technology is the promise of faster development and reduced maintenance costs. In traditional systems, ongoing maintenance costs amount to more than 80% of the overall cost of the system. Object-oriented systems promise to reduce maintenance costs through reusable objects that can dramatically reduce maintenance. In many cases, developers only need to identify an object class that functions like the object that they desire to create, and specify the differences between the object and their new object. This type of code reusability can dramatically reduce development and maintenance costs.

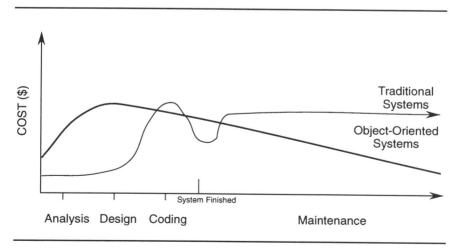

Figure 1.2.   Cost as a function of time.

Object-oriented systems make these promises:

Reduced maintenance   The primary goal of object-oriented development is the assurance that the system will enjoy a longer life while having far smaller maintenance costs. Because most of the processes within the system are encapsulated, the behaviors may be reused and incorporated into new behaviors.

Real-world modeling   Object-oriented systems tend to model the real world in a more complete fashion than do traditional methods. Objects are organized into classes of objects, and objects are associated with behaviors. The model is based on objects rather than on data and processing.

Improved reliability   Object-oriented systems promise to be far more reliable than traditional systems, primarily because new behaviors can be "built" from existing objects.

High code reusability   When a new object is created, it will automatically inherit the data attributes and characteristics of the class from which it was spawned. The new object will also inherit the data and behaviors from all superclasses in which it participates. When a user creates a new type of a widget, the new object behaves "widgetty," while having new behaviors that are defined to the system.

In many ways, the promise of reduced maintenance costs may be realized because the system allows itself to be modified and enhanced with a minimum of effort. However, when things go awry, object-oriented systems can be a nightmare to repair.

There are several features of the object-oriented paradigm that make the diagnosis and repair of problems difficult. The first problem is inheritance. When these programs fail, it can be very difficult to locate the offending line of code, because it is not clear which object physically contains the code.

While information hiding and encapsulation are a great benefit to object-oriented systems, when a problem occurs it can often become difficult to isolate the cause of the problem. Because variables are localized within the objects, and the objects are isolated into well-defined modules, the "hidden" data values are not readily apparent to the maintenance programmer, and a system dump is sometimes required in order to find the error.

Also, "multiple inheritance," the feature by which an object may inherit behaviors from many superclasses, creates diagnostic problems. Even after a problem has been located, testing a program change can be a formidable chore, because a line of code may participate in many different contexts and with many different objects. All of the possible permutations of a repaired behavior will need to be tested to ensure that a change does not spawn additional problems.

It should be noted that the object-oriented method is an approach to problem solving, and is *not* a tool, a product, or a type of technology. In fact, extensions of existing languages may make many 4GLs (and even some 3GLs) into OOPLs. The fourth-generation languages of C++, OOREX, and Visual Basic® are excellent examples of object-oriented extensions to classical programming languages.

Object-oriented systems are derived from a rigorous method, and although there are many procedural languages that have object-oriented extensions, there is no need to invest in new software in order to benefit from the object technology approach. Many of the "classical" programming languages such as FORTRAN and ADA support some of the basic constructs necessary for object-oriented programming. Many commercial databases can also be customized to adhere to the object technology approach.

Even some of the most "Precambrian" programming languages such as FORTRAN can benefit from an object-oriented method. While not "pure" according to the theoreticians, it is better to use some of the major benefits of the object technology approach, even with a classical language. For example, the FORTRAN language supports subroutines that may be entered from many points, not just from the subroutine header. This allows the simulation of encapsulation (Meyer, 1988).

The same point applies to the use of existing commercial databases. If an object technology approach can yield some major benefits, then it is a moot point that an object-oriented implementation is not "pure" from a theoretical standpoint.

In the object technology model, database entities are called "classes." Specific instances of a class are called "objects." "Class instances" and "objects" are terms that are used interchangeably in object-oriented jargon. One must note that not all classes will have instances (objects). In a class hierarchy, only the lowest level of classes may have instances, while the superclasses exist only to maintain data and behaviors that the object will inherit from these classes.

The problem with a standard definition of an object-oriented paradigm was predicted by Rentsch (1982) when he stated, ". . . Everyone will be in favor of it. Every manufacturer will promote his products as supporting it. Every manager will pay lip service to it. Every programmer will practice it (differently), and no one will know what it is." Rentsch's prophecy has been fulfilled. The theoreticians today continue to hotly debate the characteristics of object-oriented "things," whether they are databases, programming languages, or everyday objects (pun intended). I recently noticed a research paper titled, "My cat is object-oriented."

1.6. CHARACTERISTICS OF THE OBJECT-ORIENTED APPROACH

There are several properties that theoreticians claim a system must possess in order to be called object-oriented. In the real world, many of these properties are only viewed as suggestions, as evidenced by the popular object-oriented language SmallTalk, which does not support multiple inheritance.

1.6.1. Abstraction

Abstraction is defined as the conceptual (*not* concrete) existence of classes within the database. For example, a database may have a class hierarchy that includes classes having no objects. A military database may contain the conceptual entities of DIVISION, BATTALION, SQUADRON, and PLATOON. The function of the database is to track the platoons, and the entity classes of DIVISION, BATTALION, and SQUADRON may not have any associated objects. This is not to say that there is no purpose for abstract classes. When a class is defined, it is associated with behaviors, and these behaviors will be inherited by each object in the PLA-TOON class. From a database perspective, there will be no instances of any objects except PLATOON, but higher levels in the class hierarchy will contain behaviors that the PLATOON objects inherit.

1.6.2.   Abstract Data Types

UniSQL, a relational/object-oriented database developed by Dr. Wong Kim (1990), supports the concept of nested tables, whereby a data "field" in a table may be a range of values or an entire table. This concept is called complex, or unstructured, data typing. With this approach the domain of values for a specific field in a relational database may be defined. This ability to "nest" data tables allows for relationship data to be incorporated directly into the table structure. For example, the OCCUPATIONS field in the table establishes a one-to-many relationship between an employee and his or her valid occupations. Also note the ability to nest the entire SKILLS table within a single field. In this example, only valid skills may reside in the SKILLS field; this implements the relational concept of "domain integrity."

1.6.3.   Inheritance

Inheritance is defined as the ability of a lower-level object to inherit, or access, the data items and behaviors associated with all classes above it in the class hierarchy. For example, consider a scenario where a many-to-many relationship exists between ORDER and ITEM classes. Because an order may be for many items, and an item participates in many orders, these entities form the classic many-to-many relationship. It is necessary to establish some kind of linkage between these entities to allow for an order to have many items and an item to participate in many orders. For example, when an order is placed, a junction class called ORDER_LINE is invoked, and an object is created to link the item with the order. The behaviors of this ORDER_LINE object will be different depending on the data items and behaviors inherited from its ORDER and ITEM superclasses.

Data inheritance can affect behavior. For example, if the ITEM

Traditional Tables:

(Fields contain single values)

Name	Sex	Phone
Jones	M	333-1234
Smyth	F	444-3836

Tables with Abstract Data Types:

(Fields may contain lists or entire tables)

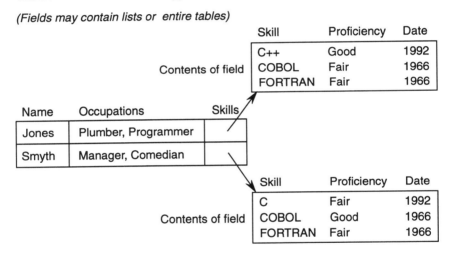

Figure 1.3.   Abstraction.

record has an existing inventory level equal to zero, the order will be rejected. For inherited behavior, the PLACE_ORDER behavior (associated with the ORDER class) may be either RUSH or REGULAR, and the presence of the attributes RUSH or REGULAR affect the PLACE_ORDER behavior.

Multiple inheritance refers to the ability of an object to inherit attributes and behaviors from more than one superclass.

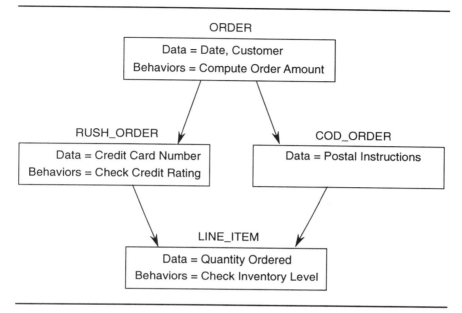

Figure 1.4.   Inheritance.

This ability is especially useful for "junction" objects that establish a many-to-many relationship between two classes. For example, a line-item object will inherit from two classes: an ORDER class, which may be RUSH or COD, and the ITEM class, which may be perishable or nonperishable.

For example, the many-to-many relationship between an ORDER class and the ITEM class is established with a LINE_ITEM class, which serves to link the orders with the items that participate in the order. The LINE_ITEM class would "inherit" the data item and behaviors of the ORDER class and the ITEM class. When a LINE_ITEM record is added to the database, the behaviors from the order and the item objects are invoked.

1.6.4.   Polymorphism

Polymorphism is the ability of different objects to receive the same message and behave in different ways. This concept has

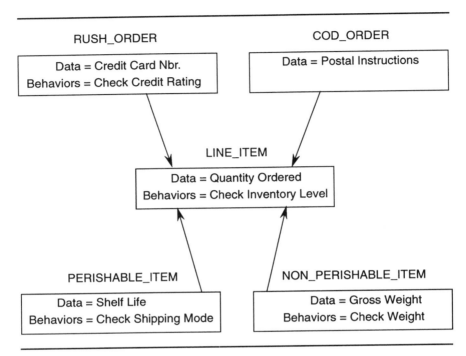

Figure 1.5.   Multiple inheritance.

many parallels in the real world. An event—say, a volcanic eruption—may have many different effects on the livings things in the area, with the poisonous gases killing all air-breathing animals while at the same time nourishing the small marine organisms nearby. The single behavior, ERUPTION, has had different effects upon objects within the ANIMAL class. Another analogy can be found in the business world. For a personnel manager, the event of PROMOTION will cause different behaviors depending on the class of EMPLOYEE that receives the PROMOTION. MANAGEMENT objects will receive stock options and country club memberships, which are not offered to JANITOR objects.

The concept of polymorphism came from the programming concept of "overloading." Overloading refers to the ability of a programming function to perform more than one type of operation depending on the context in which the function is used. For example, consider the following BASIC program:

```
REM Sample BASIC program to show polymorphism

REM Increment the counter

COUNTER=COUNTER+1

REM Concatenate the string

N$ = "Mr. Burleson"
S$ = "Hello there, " + N$

END
```

In this example, the operator "+" is used to indicate addition in one context and concatenation in another context. But what determines the way that the operator will function? Clearly, the BASIC compiler knows that the "+" operator means addition when it is used in the context where a number is passed as an argument, and it knows that concatenation is required when character strings are passed as an argument to the operator.

The implications of polymorphism are that a standard interface may be created for a related group of objects. The specific action performed by the object will depend on the message passed to the interface. Because the programmer is no longer concerned with the internal constructs of the object, extremely complex programs can be created. The programmer only needs to understand the interface to use the object.

In the real world, polymorphism can be described by looking at standard interfaces. In most PC-based software the F1 key has a special meaning. Pressing F1 will invoke a context-sensitive help function, and explain the function to the user. These help functions have vastly different methods and different data storage techniques, but the standard interface, F1, is polymorphic and invokes different internal mechanisms depending on the software.

Another example is the controls on an automobile. While the internal workings of automobiles are vastly different, the steering wheels are always round, and the gas pedal is always to the right of the brake. These polymorphic interfaces make it possible for any person to drive a car without being concerned with the underlying structures of the vehicle.

All communication between objects and their behaviors is accomplished with "messages" that are passed as behaviors. For example, consider two objects, RUSH_ORDER and COD_ORDER, that belong to the ORDER class.

When a message such as PREPARE_INVOICE is called, it may contain sub-behaviors such as PREPARE_INVOICE and COMPUTE_CHARGES. The message PREPARE_INVOICE directs the system to compute the shipping charges. The message will cause different procedures to be invoked depending on whether the receiving object is a RUSH_ORDER object or a COD_ORDER object, even if they are both objects within the ORDER class. A rush order would include overnight mail calculations and the COD order would contain additional computations for the total amount due. This is equivalent to the following procedural language code:

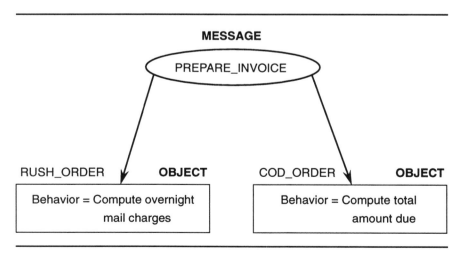

Figure 1.6.   Polymorphism.

1. Object-oriented call:

```
PLACE_ORDER(PREPARE_INVOICE(COMPUTE_CHARGES))
```

2. Procedural language equivalent:

```
IF (RUSH_ORDER)

          COMPUTE SHIPPING = TOT_AMNT * .25

     ELSE

          COMPUTE SHIPPING = TOT_AMNT * .10

     IF (COD_ORDER)

          COMPUTE TOT_DUE = TOT_AMNT + SHIPPING

     ELSE

          COMPUTE TOT_DUE = 0
```

1.6.5. Encapsulation

Encapsulation means that each object within the system has a well-defined interface with distinct borders. In plain English, encapsulation refers to the "localized variables" that may be used within an object behavior and cannot be referenced outside of that behavior. This closely parallels the concept of information hiding. Encapsulation also ensures that all updates to the database are performed using, or by way of, the behaviors associated with the database objects.

Code and data can be enclosed together into a "black box," and these "boxes" may then function independently of all other objects within the system. From a programming perspective, an object is an encapsulated routine of data and behaviors. Objects may contain "public" variables, which are used to handle the interfaces to the object, and "private" variables, which are known only to the object. Once created, an object is treated as a variable of its own type. For example, an object of class CAR is created as a routine with a data type called CAR, and is treated as a compound variable by the program.

Encapsulation is used in nondatabase object-oriented applications to ensure that all operations are performed through the programmer-defined interface, and that data will never be modified outside of the application shell. But what about ad hoc query and update? It appears that any declarative database language such as SQL, which allows "external" retrieval and update, does not follow the dictates of encapsulation and is therefore inconsistent with object-oriented database management.

For example, a relational database could be defined to have a behavior called ADD_LINE_ITEM, which serves to check inventory levels for an item and add an item to an order only if sufficient stock is available. This behavior ensures that orders are not entered for out-of-stock items. With a language such as SQL, the object-oriented behavior could be bypassed, and LINE_ITEM records could be added without any regard for inventory levels.

Because encapsulation and SQL are clearly incompatible, the only conclusion that can be reached is that either:

1. Encapsulation does not apply to object-oriented databases because declarative languages violate the principle.
2. Declarative languages cannot be used within a true object-oriented database.

I will present a solution to this dilemma in the chapter on SQL and object technology principles.

1.6.6. Extensibility

Extensibility is the ability of an object-oriented system to add new behaviors to an existing system without changing the application shell. This is an especially powerful concept and allows an object-oriented database to handle novel data situations.

For example, consider a customer database. We may have preexisting definitions of the CUSTOMER class and two defined objects within this class, say, NEW_CUSTOMER and REGULAR_CUSTOMER. With an extensible database, new ob-

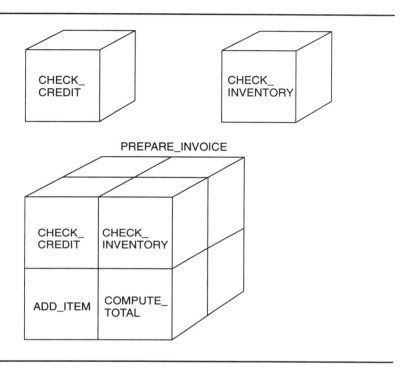

Figure 1.7.   Encapsulation: independent "black boxes" allow for nesting behaviors.

jects may be created for any class, and the appropriate behaviors can be associated with the new object.

Assume that we are creating a new object, PREFERRED_ CUSTOMER. The extensible database would allow us to create this new object, specifying the unique data attributes of this object and creating the behaviors for PREFERRED _CUSTOMER(s). Once defined, PREFERRED_CUSTOMER may be referenced in the same fashion as any other objects within the database schema.

Extensible databases also allow for predefined data attributes and behaviors to be reused as new objects are created. For a detailed discussion of extensibility, see Chapter 5, Designing Dynamic Class Hierarchies.

1.7. BENEFITS OF THE OBJECT-ORIENTED APPROACH

1. **Reduced maintenance costs.** Behaviors are stored within the database and are isolated from the application. Because each "method" is encapsulated, building blocks are created that may be recombined to create new behaviors.
2. **Improved flexibility.** Because objects can be dynamically called and accessed, new objects may be created at any time. The new objects may inherit data attributes from one or many other objects. Behaviors may be inherited from superclasses, and novel behaviors may be added without affecting existing systems functions.

There are several important differences between the object technology approach to problem solving and traditional data processing systems. The first, and most important, is the absolute necessity of proper analysis before implementation. Some of the fourth-generation languages are designed to allow developers to create their systems in an ad hoc fashion, building screens and database tables without any formal forethought. This approach with object-oriented development is dangerous. While a properly designed class hierarchy will have very low maintenance, it is not easily modified in an object-oriented environment. Great care must be taken to properly identify the classes and the relationships between the classes, and all one-to-many, many-to-many, and ISA relationships must be properly identified. Most object technology systems do not lend themselves to class modification after coding has begun, and caution must be taken to ensure that the initial design is correct.

There are several major misconceptions that must be addressed when considering the use of an object-oriented method.

1. **Object-oriented development is not a panacea.** Object-oriented development is best suited for dynamic, interactive environments, as evidenced by its widespread acceptance in CAD/CAM and engineering design systems. Wide-scale object-oriented corporate systems are still unproved, and many bread-and-butter information systems applications (i.e., pay-

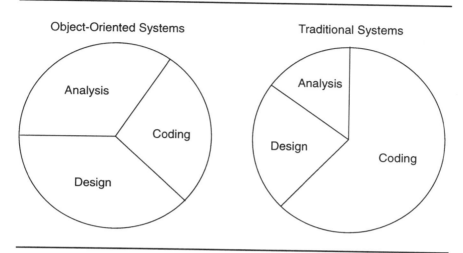

Figure 1.8.   Object-oriented systems require more analysis and design effort than traditional systems.

roll, accounting) may not benefit from the object-oriented approach.

2. **Object-oriented development is not a technology.** Although many advocates are religious in their fervor for object-oriented systems, remember that all the hoopla is directed at the object-oriented approach to problem solving and not to any specific technology.

3. **Object-oriented development is not yet completely accepted by major vendors.** Object-oriented development has gained some market respectability, and vendors have gone from catering to a "lunatic fringe" to a respected market. Still, there are major reservations as to whether object-oriented development will become a major force or fade into history, as in the 1980s when decision support systems (DSS) made great promises, only to fade into obscurity.

When one investigates the general acceptance of object-oriented systems in the commercial marketplace, you generally find that most managers would like to see an object technology approach, but they do not have the time to train their staffs in object-oriented methods. Others will say that the object-oriented method is only for graphical workstation systems, and that there is no pressing need for object-oriented systems within mainstream business systems.

Even though commercial object-oriented programming languages have been on the market for several years, systems written with object-oriented languages comprise less than 1% of systems today.

Once a major vendor begins conforming to a standard, it can become impossible to retrofit their standard to conform to another standard. When the American Standards Committee came out with a standard character set for computers (ASCII), IBM disregarded the standard and proceeded with their own character set, called the Extended Binary Character Data Interchange Code (EBCDIC). Even thirty years later, there has still been no resolution between ASCII and EBCDIC, and data transfers between ASCII and EBCDIC machines continue to present problems. For example, EBCDIC has no characters for open/close bracket ([]), and ASCII has no character for the cent sign(¢).

These same types of problems may plague object-oriented databases, except to a much larger degree. As we know, vendors have a vested interest in proprietary software and methods, and they are very reluctant to conform to any standard that may have the result of declining use of their product. Mega-vendors such as Microsoft also have the clout to overwhelm a marketplace with any standard they choose, much as IBM did with the EBCDIC character set. As systems move more toward an open architecture, the interfaces between one object-oriented database and another may not be seamless. For example, one object-oriented database standard may support multiple inheritance while another may only support single inheritance.

PROBLEMS AND EXERCISES

1. The concepts of polymorphism and multiple inheritance are sometimes misunderstood. Find two examples of polymorphism and two examples of multiple inheritance, and describe the differences between these concepts.

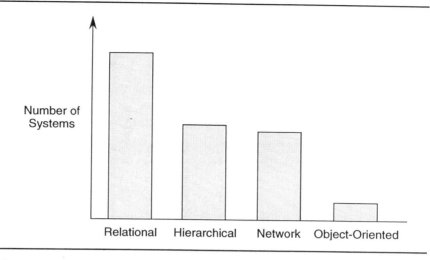

Figure 1.9.   Database usage by type of architecture.

2. Abstraction is a principle that can be applied to some traditional programming languages. Show how an abstract data type could be implemented in a COBOL working-storage definition, and in a PASCAL data definition.
3. Briefly describe the conditions that led to the development of the object technology approach, and elaborate about why there is no general consensus on standards regarding object-oriented principles and databases.
4. Give three specific examples of application systems that would not benefit from object technology. Justify your reasons for excluding these systems.
5. Describe how systems development efforts will change when using an object-oriented method. Explain the staffing and training considerations that would not be encountered with the development of a traditional database system.
6. Explain why object-oriented development will reduce the maintenance costs for a system. How can flexibility sometimes be a hindrance when fixing program bugs?
7. Many advocates of object technology state that within the next fifteen years, all development will eventually follow an

object-oriented methodology. Elaborate upon why you agree or disagree with this statement.

REFERENCES

Ahad, R., Dedo, D., "OpenDB from Hewlett-Packard: a commercial object-oriented database system," *Journal of Object-Oriented Programming*, Vol. 4, Issue 9, Feb. 1992.

Ahmed, S., Wong, A., Sriram, D., Logcher, R., "A comparison of object-oriented database management systems for engineering applications," MIT Technical Report IESL-90-03, 1990.

Babcock, C., "Object Lessons," *Computerworld*, May 3rd, 1993.

Banciinon, F., *Building an Object-Oriented Database System: The Story of O2* (San Mateo, CA: Morgan Kaufman Publishers, 1992).

Bradley, J., "An object-relationship diagrammatic technique for object-oriented database definitions," *Journal of Database Administration*, Vol. 3, Issue 2, Spring 1992.

Brown, A.W., *Object-Oriented Databases and Their Applications to Software Engineering* (New York: McGraw-Hill, 1991).

Cattell, R.G.G., *Object Data Management: Object-Oriented and Extended Relational Database Systems* (Reading, MA: Addison-Wesley, 1991).

Cattel, R.G.G., Rogers, T., "Combining object-oriented and Relational models of data," International Workshop on Object-Oriented Database Systems, Proceedings, Wash., DC, IEEE Computer Society Press, 1986.

Date, C.J., *An Introduction to Database Systems* (Reading, MA: Addison-Wesley, 1990).

De Troyer, O., Keustermans, J., Meersman, R., "How helpful is object-oriented language for an object-oriented database model?," International Workshop on Object-Oriented Database Systems, Proceedings, Wash., DC, IEEE Computer Society Press, 1986.

Dittrich, K., Dayal, U., Buchmann, P., *On Object-Oriented Database Systems* (New York: Springer-Verlag Publishers, 1991).

Gorman, K., Choobineh, J., "An overview of the object-oriented entity relationship model (OOERM)," Proceedings of the Twenty-Third Annual Hawaii International Conference on Information Systems (Vol. 3), 336–345, 1991.

Kim, W., *Introduction to Object-Oriented Databases* (Cambridge, MA: The MIT Press, 1990).

McFadden, F., Hoffer, J., *Database Management* (Menlo Park, CA: Benjamin Cummings Publishing Company, 1987).

Melton, J., "The MOOSE is loose," *Database Programming & Design*, May 1993.

Meyer, B., *Object-Oriented Software Construction* (Englewood Cliffs, NJ: Prentice-Hall, 1988).

Rentsch, B., "Object Oriented Programming Issues," Communications of the ACM, July 1982.

Soloviev, V., "An overview of three commercial object-oriented database management systems: ONTOS, Objectstore, and O/sub 2/," *SIGMOD Record*, Vol. 21, March 1992.

Stone, C., "The rise of object databases: can the Object Management Group get database vendors to agree on object standards?," *DBMS*, July 1992.

Thalheim, B., "Extending the entity-relationship model for a high-level, theory-based database design," International Workshop on Object-Oriented Database Systems, Proceedings, Wash., DC, IEEE Computer Society Press, March 1990.

Unland, R., Schlageter, G., "Object-oriented database systems: concepts and perspectives," International Workshop on Object-Oriented Database Systems, Proceedings, Wash., DC, IEEE Computer Society Press, 1990.

Yourdon, E., "The marriage of relational and object-oriented design," *Relational Journal*, Vol. 3, Issue 6, Jan. 1992.

Varma, S., "Object-oriented databases: where are we now?," *Database Programming & Design*, May 1993.

Object-Oriented
Database Management

2.1.   INTRODUCTION

Before the introduction of commercial object-oriented databases, object-oriented systems were rather primitive. Industrial-strength commercial database software offers features such as data recovery, 24×7 availability, and client-server capability. The area of object-oriented database (OODB) is growing at a phenomenal rate. In 1992 the revenue from object-oriented databases was approximately $10 million, but by 1997 object-oriented databases are expected to grow into a $90 million per year industry. International Data Corporation (IDC) estimates that the market for object-oriented databases may be as high as $446 million by 1996.

Most large companies recognize the benefits of object-oriented techniques, but they must deal with the reality of "legacy" systems, some of which consist of hundreds of programs and have taken decades to create.

After an organization has recognized the benefits of the object technology approach, there are several migration paths:

PATH 1. Twin Database Architectures. Object-oriented databases are chosen for applications that would most benefit from the architecture, while relational databases continue to be

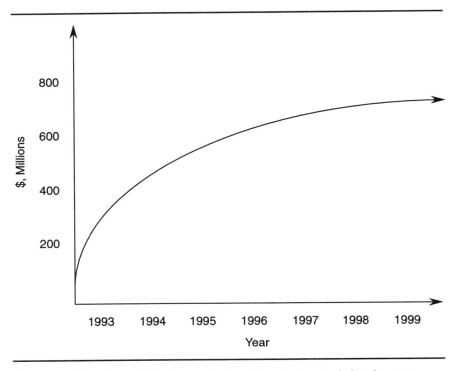

Figure 2.1.   Predicted growth for object-oriented databases.

used for systems that need the ad hoc capability of SQL. For example, marketing systems generally have few object classes, but they have a tremendous need for "what if" simulation. An object-oriented database would probably be a poor choice for this type of application. On the other hand, a graphical tool for developing automobile parts would be an ideal fit for object technology.

PATH 2. Bridge Building. Communications are established between object-oriented databases and existing databases.

A. **Use object technology with relational databases**—Object-oriented "front-ends" are used to access information in various types of databases, including relational, network, and hierarchical. Numerous products such as UniSQL® allow object-oriented systems to access relational databases. The

Object-Oriented Systems Talk to Relational Database

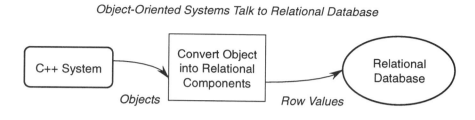

Relational Systems Talk to Object-Oriented Database

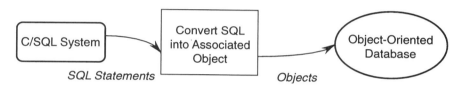

Figure 2.2.   Database coexistence methods.

object request is broken down into its relational components, which are then passed to the relational database for retrieval.

B. **Use relational access to object-oriented databases—** This scenario involves the use of a "reassembler," which interrogates the SQL request and determines which objects contain the desired data items. The object is then retrieved and disassembled into the desired items.

2.2.   THE PROBLEM WITH OBJECT-ORIENTED DATA PERSISTENCE

Let me start with the unpopular assertion that object-oriented data storage, as it exists today in "home-rolled" databases, is a quantum leap backwards in database technology. Many programmers of C++ create their own linked-list data structures to achieve object persistence, and bypass the inherent benefits of a database manager.

Object-oriented databases perform far faster than relational databases because of their use of pointers. In object-oriented databases, pointers are used to establish the relationships between objects. Relational databases also use internal pointers for indexing, but the relationships between tables are established by inserting redundant data items. Ad hoc queries (i.e., those queries that are not predefined in a class hierarchy) cannot be performed without restructuring the records to add pointers for the new relationships.

These "home-rolled" object-oriented databases are generally unique to each application, and they seldom contain concurrency control, a data dictionary, or a recovery mechanism. Even more important, these link-list structures require complex navigation to access the objects. This approach is not the only solution. With proper design, existing relational databases may be used with many of the features of object technology.

There are three ways to create an object-oriented database:

1. Use a OODBMS.
2. Write your own systems with in C++.
3. Extend the relational database model to support objects.

Object-oriented systems allow for the dynamic creation of new objects and are very well suited for graphical applications such as Computer Aided Systems Engineering (CASE) and Computer Aided Design (CAD). However, most traditional business databases have static data structures and do not usually require the ability to "self-define" new object classes.

Most of the systems in the business environment are created for basic business functions such as accounting and manufacturing. These systems are very static in their data requirements and would seldom, if ever, require any changes to their underlying entities. The most abstract features of object technology systems, such as multiple inheritance, would not be required for most business applications.

Another benefit of "pure" object-oriented databases is their tremendous speed. Because object technology systems use embedded pointers to establish their data relationships, they will almost always outperform a relational database, but they attain

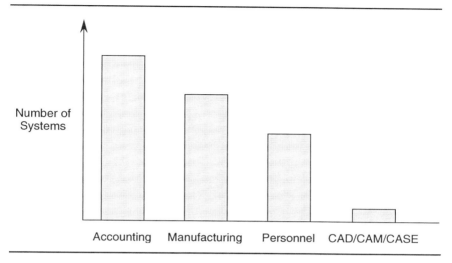

Figure 2.3.   Database usage by type of application.

this speed by sacrificing the ability to dynamically establish new relationships between existing database records. In other words, object-oriented databases achieve their speed at the expense of data independence. In a relational database, information is "assembled" from independent tables at the time of the query. Object-oriented advocates state that this approach is analogous to assembling your automobile when you want to travel, and then disassembling the car after you have completed your trip. An object technology system preestablishes each of the data relationships with embedded pointers.

The requirements of an object-oriented design pose some very specific challenges for the designer who wishes to incorporate object-oriented functionality into a relational database. The database must support a well-defined class hierarchy, maintain the data requirements of different objects, and handle the inheritance of behaviors within the class hierarchy. In fact, many of the more advanced object-oriented features such as polymorphism and multiple inheritance can be incorporated into a relational database design. Bear in mind that many, if not most, real-world applications of object-oriented databases will not require the ad-

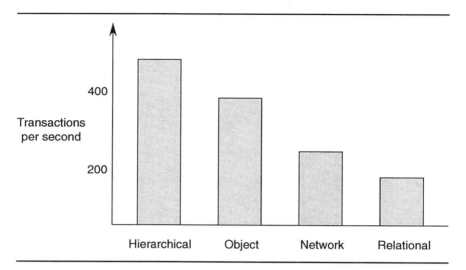

Figure 2.4.   Relative speeds of the database architectures.

vanced features of the object-oriented paradigm, such as multiple inheritance.

Today there are many vendors offering object-oriented database software, and there are new offerings almost every month. As of May 1993, the most popular object-oriented databases include:

Atriom®	by Atriom Incorporated, Waltham, MA
ENVY/Developer®	by Object Technology International Incorporated, Ottawa, Canada
Gemstone®	by Servio Corporation, Alameda, CA
Itasca®	by Itasca Systems, Minneapolis, MN
Objectivity/DB®	by Objectivity, Menlo Park, CA
ObjectStore®	by Object Design, Incorporated, Burlington, MA
Ontos®	by Ontologic, Burlington, MA
OpenODB®	by Hewlett-Packard, Palo Alto, CA
VERSANT®	by Versant Object Technology, Menlo Park, CA

As of 1993, object-oriented databases serve a very small market (about 2%) of the overall database market, and this market primarily consists of very dynamic workstation applications. But what about the other 98% of the database market? Why don't large corporations abandon their relational databases to invest in object technology software?

The answer to this question is not simple. While the goals of object technology are very desirable, many database designers do not see a way that an object technology approach can be adopted without sacrificing the features enjoyed by commercial database systems. Some large vendor companies, such as IBM, state that the relational database model is completely incompatible with the object-oriented approach, and that they have no plans to create "hybrid" databases, which combine the features of relational and object technology. However, IBM has recently announced that future releases of the DB2 database will offer support for some object-oriented methods, including the ability to self-define new data types.

But let's review the benefits of object-oriented systems. Commonly used procedures can be reused in a relational database by establishing "triggers," or database request modules (DBRMs), that can be "fired" at specific database events, such as the insertion or modification of a record. Object-oriented systems also promise that an object can inherit the data attributes of its superclass. This can also be achieved in a relational database by using a trigger to join the required tables.

Polymorphism, the ability of objects to react differently to an identical message, can also be modeled in a relational database. Multiple inheritance, whereby an object inherits data and behaviors from more than one superclass, can also be replicated in a relational database. In fact, the only object-oriented feature that a relational database cannot model is the ability to define abstract data types. A relational table cannot be defined where a single field contains multiple values, or an array of values. However, it is not necessary to fully adhere to the object-oriented paradigm in order to benefit from its methods, and many of the features of the object technology paradigm are not necessary for corporate databases.

2.3.   OBJECT-ORIENTED VS. CLASSICAL DATABASES

Database management systems, as we define them today, evolved out of a need within the computer community for a united set of data structures that can handle their information in a cohesive manner.

Object-oriented toolsets such as Versant by Object Technology, advertise that it is a "feature" (read "bug that we can't fix"), that the database manager is tightly coupled with the programming environment. Mary Loomis, the vice president of Versant Technical Services, states, "Because an ODBMS is tightly integrated with an object programming language, a single model or paradigm is used for both persistent and transient data. The result is fewer lines of code than if a file system or RDBMS were used for persistent storage, and fewer lines of code nearly always translates into increased productivity and improved quality" (Loomis, 1991).

In reality, tightly coupling the database with the procedural language can be a major drawback. Looking back to the 1960s, when flat-file data was tightly coupled with the programming languages, we see that horrendous problems ensued. This "feature" of flat-file environments was one of the major reasons that the first commercial database systems were developed. A future goal of object-oriented databases is to produce systems that are language-independent, so that any language may have embedded object-oriented statements. The ultimate goal would be to have fourth-generation languages (4GL), which could directly access the object database.

Regardless of the sophistication of a database manager, it remains true that all databases are constructed from simple data structures such as linked-lists, B-trees, and hashed files. In reviewing the building blocks of database systems, it is possible to gain a historical perspective on the evolution of database, and to remember the past, so that we are not condemned to repeat it.

The following pages are a historical review of database evolution, showing each of the enhancements that were introduced with each new architecture. It is also important to review the problems inherent to each database architecture. As you will see, there are striking similarities between object-oriented databases and earlier database architectures. By understanding the historical reason that object-oriented databases have evolved into their present form, we can gain insight into the future trend and directions of databases.

2.3.1. Flat-File Systems   2200 B.C.–1965 A.D.

Prior to the development of the early commercial databases such as IMS, many "database" systems were a conglomeration of flat-file storage methods. The term "flat-file" includes physical-sequential storage as well as the indexed sequential access method (ISAM) and virtual sequential access method (VSAM). For physical-sequential file systems, updates are performed by rewriting

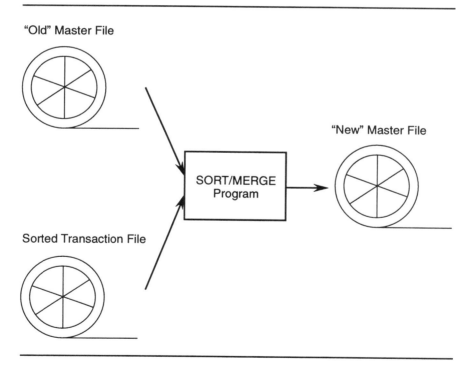

Figure 2.5.   Physical sequential files are updated by the creation of a "new" file.

the master file, and data access could only be performed sequentially. Other flat-file systems such as ISAM and VSAM were physical-sequential files with indexes, and were stored on disks or drums.

The data access methods used by these systems were very primitive. The BDAM (Basic Direct Access Method) was used for fast access and retrieval of information. BDAM uses a "hashing algorithm," which converts a symbolic key into a location address on disk (a disk address). Unfortunately, the range of addresses generated by these algorithms requires careful management. Because a hashing algorithm always produces the same key each time it reads an input value, duplicate keys have to be avoided. BDAM file structures also consume a large amount of disk storage. Because records are randomly distributed across the disk device, it is common to see hashed files with more unused spaces than occupied space. In most cases, a BDAM file is considered "logically" full if more than 70% of the space contains data records.

Despite these problems, hashing remains one of the fastest ways to store and retrieve information. Most mainframe systems can convert a symbolic key into a disk address in as little as 50 milliseconds. Although hashing is a very old technique, it is still a very powerful method. Many C++ programmers use hashing to store and retrieve records within their object-oriented applications.

It is interesting that in 1993, more data is stored in physical-sequential format than in all of the other file formats. Companies continue to use a flat-file architecture because of systems that contain large amounts of unchanging, infrequently used data. Magnetic tapes, which are 10,000 times cheaper than disk, are still the most economical way to store large volumes of data.

Overall, online systems using ISAM and VSAM data structures were very difficult to create. Programmers were forced to write all of the details of the pseudo-conversational tasks, and it was very difficult to create complex transaction processing systems. The problems inherent in these systems were very serious, and an effort was undertaken to rethink the entire concept of data storage. The problems included the following:

Data relationships could not be maintained. Early flat-file systems could not easily recognize and manage the natural

STORE CUSTOMER WHERE CUST-KEY = "Burleson"

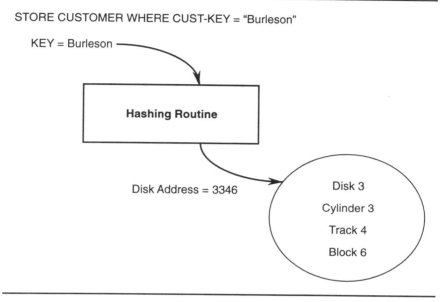

Figure 2.6.   Hashed file storage: a symbolic key is used to quickly generate a unique disk address.

relationships between data items. One-to-many and many-to-many data relationships were often ignored, and widespread denormalization of the data occurred.

"Islands of information" developed within organizations, as different departments developed independent flat-file systems. These departmental "islands" were often written in different programming languages, with different file structures, and it was very difficult for a department to share information with other departments.

Widespread data redundancy developed. Each department within the corporate database often duplicated information, leading to increased costs of data storage, as well as the possibility of update anomalies, occurring when a item was changed within one department but not within another.

Maintenance nightmares ensued. Because these systems had no repository of "metadata," program changes became very cumbersome. Whenever a file changed in structure, the programs that referred to the file could not readily be identified, and every program that referenced that file had to be modified and recompiled.

Tightly coupled data and programs led to maintenance problems. Because many application programs defined and maintained their own data structures, there was a problem as all new programs were forced to adhere to the calling procedures of the existing programs. The same communications problems exist within object-oriented systems. The CORBA standard for object-oriented systems was designed to ensure that this problem will not resurface in the 1990s.

There was no concurrency control or recovery mechanisms. Systems had no method for simultaneous updating of information, and no way to "roll-forward" information in case of disk failure.

There was no method for establishing relationships between data items. The relationships between data items are generally lost, or introduced with cumbersome data structures such as repeating fields within the records.

2.3.2.   The Hierarchical Database   c. 1965–1993 A.D.

The problems associated with flat-file systems led to development of the first commercial database offering, IMS® (Information Management System) from IBM. IMS is considered a "hierarchical" database, and IMS is well suited for modeling systems in which the entities are composed of descending one-to-many relationships. Relationships are established with "child" and "twin" pointers, and these pointers are embedded into the prefix of every record in the database.

IMS has concurrency control and a backup and recovery mechanism. The recovery mechanism stored "before" and "after" images of each record that was changed, and these images could be used to "roll-back" the database if a transaction failed to complete, or "roll-forward," in case of a disk failure. IMS could be used with CICS, and developers began to create the first online

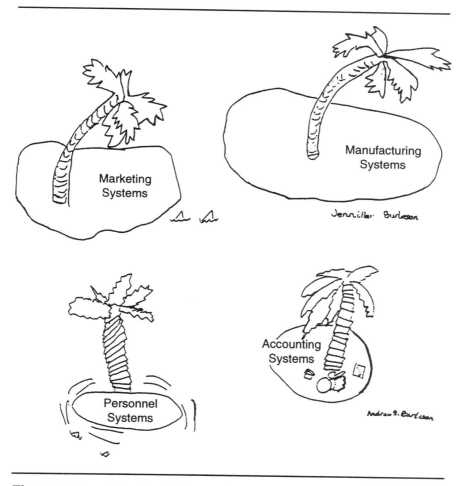

Figure 2.7.   Islands of information.

database systems for the mainframe. But IMS had several major drawbacks. While IMS is very good at modeling hierarchical data relationships, complex data relationships such as many-to-many and recursive many-to-many (bill-of-material) relationships had to be implemented in a very clumsy fashion, with the use of "phantom" records. The IMS database also suffers from its complexity. Learning to program and administer an IMS database

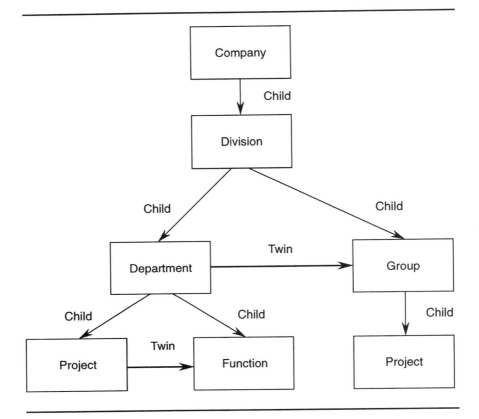

Figure 2.8.   Hierarchical database architecture: child/twin pointers establish relationships.

requires months of training; consequently, IMS development remains very slow and cumbersome.

Who has the "fastest" database?

While IMS is considered a dinosaur by today's standards, IBM continues to sell new copies of IMS, and IMS is still used by hundreds of corporations. While some of these are "legacy systems," which are not easily converted to modern technology, many continue to use IMS because of its high speed. A hybrid of IMS, called IMS/FASTPATH®, is one of the fastest commercial databases available, even by today's standards. IMS/FASTPATH is used at companies that may have hundreds or even thousands of concurrent transactions, and some IMS configurations have surpassed the 1000 transactions per second barrier.

2.3.3. The CODASYL Network Database   c. 1970–1980 A.D.

Many of the problems associated with flat-file systems were partially addressed with the introduction of the IMS database product by IBM, but there remained no published standard for commercial database systems. The Committee on Development of Applied Symbolic Languages (CODASYL) formed a database task group (the DBTG) to address database standards. The CODASYL DBTG was commissioned to develop a set of "rules," or a model, for database management systems, just as the ODMG group is doing with object-oriented databases. The CODASYL DBTG developed what is called the "network model" for databases. Among other things, the CODASYL DBTG decided that:

1. The term "data base" was improper, and "database" was correct.
2. A framework for a "data dictionary" would be created. The data dictionary was designed to store all metadata, including information about the database entities, relationships between entities, and information about how programs use the database.
3. A standard architecture for database systems would be used. This architecture was based on a combination of the BDAM (direct access) and linked-list data structures.
4. A separation of the logical structure of the data from the physical access methods would be maintained. For example, a programmer could state OBTAIN CALC CUSTOMER WHERE CUST-ID = "IBM" without having to worry about where the record was physically stored on the disk.
5. Procedures for concurrency control and database recovery

would be developed. Databases would manage record locks, preventing information overlaying, and databases could be rolled-forward or rolled-back, thereby ensuring data integrity.

6. A conceptual "Schema" would be described. The purpose of a schema is to govern the definition of the data and relationships. This was called DDL (Data Definition Language), and was used to describe the business model. DDL included the constructs of Files, Areas, Records, Sets, and Indexes. The term "Set" was used to name a data relationship and to describe the owner and member records in the relationship. Another construct was the Subschema. Subschemas were used as a method for creating "user views" of the overall database and were also used to enforce system security.

7. A standard data interface would be used. This was called DML (Data Manipulation Language), and covered all selection and update operations that could be performed. DML verbs include:

RETRIEVAL	Get, Find, Obtain
UPDATE	Store, Modify, Delete
CURRENCY	Disconnect, Connect, Find Current of Record-type

The CODASYL model became the framework for new commercial database systems such as the IDMS database from Cullinane Corporation, and the MDBS2 database.

While the network model was very good at representing complex data relationships, it had one major drawback. The internal data structures were not transparent to the programmer, and the programmers were required to "navigate" the database structure to extract their information. Unlike a declarative language such as SQL, a network database programmer would be required to specify the "access path," describing all of the records and the "sets" that would be used to satisfy the request.

A diagram tool to represent the data structures required by the CODASYL model was popularized by Charles Bachman, and his graphical depiction of the database schema became known as the Bachman diagram, or data structure diagram. In the Bachman

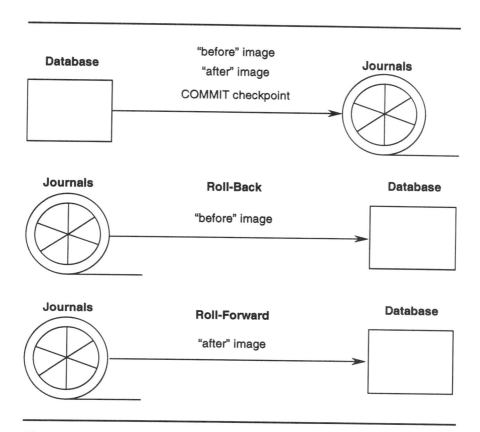

Figure 2.9.   Journals allow data integrity.

diagram, records are represented as boxes and the arrows represent relationships.

The CODASYL model combines two data storage methods to create an engine that can process hundreds of transactions per second. The CODASYL model uses the basic direct access method (BDAM), which utilizes a hashing algorithm (sometime called a CALC algorithm) to quickly store and retrieve records. CODASYL also employs linked-list data structures, which create embedded pointers in the prefix of each occurrence of a record. These pointers are used to establish relationships between data items. These pointers are called NEXT, PRIOR, and OWNER and are refer-

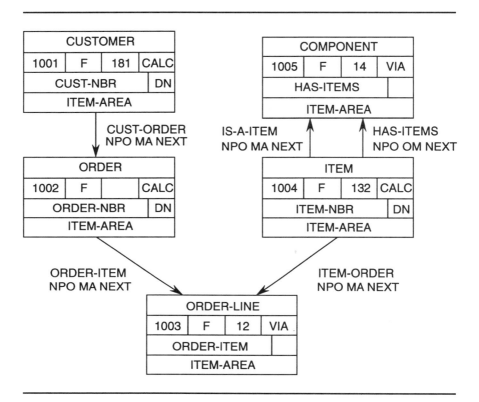

Figure 2.10. Bachman diagram.

enced in the Data Manipulation Language (DML). For example, the DML command OBTAIN NEXT ORDER WITHIN CUS-TOMER-ORDER would direct the CODASYL database to look in the prefix of the current ORDER record and find the NEXT pointer for the CUSTOMER-ORDER set. The database would then access the record whose address was found at this location.

The Bachman diagram describes the physical constructs of all record types in the database, including the location modes for all records (CALC or VIA), and all of the linked-list options. Records are stored using hashing techniques, and records that are stored "CALC" use a symbolic key to determine the physical location of the record. CODASYL databases also allow for records to be clustered. Records with "VIA" indicate that they are stored on the same physical data blocks as their owner records. Data relationships are established with "sets," which link the relationships together. For example, the ORDER-LINE records are physically clustered near their ITEM records. This is indicated on the Bachman diagram where the ORDER-LINE box shows VIA as the location mode, and the ORDER-ITEM relationship as the cluster set.

There are several advantages to the CODASYL approach, primarily with performance and the ability to represent complex data relationships. In the following example, BDAM is invoked for the OBTAIN CALC CUSTOMER statement, and linked lists are used in the statement OBTAIN NEXT CUSTOMER WITHIN CUSTOMER-ORDER.

For example, to navigate a one-to-many relationship (i.e., to get all of the orders for a customer), a CODASYL programmer would enter:

```
MOVE 'IBM' to CUST-ID.
OBTAIN CALC CUSTOMER.
PERFORM ORDER-LOOP UNTIL END-OF-SET.

ORDER-LOOP.
    OBTAIN NEXT ORDER WITHIN CUSTOMER-ORDER.
    MOVE ORDER-NO TO OUT-REC.
    WRITE OUT-REC.
```

As a visual tool, the set occurrence diagram has great potential for use in object-oriented databases. The relationships between the objects are readily apparent, and the programmer can easily visualize the navigation paths. For example, in the sample diagram, you can easily see that order 123 is for 19 pads, 3 pencils, and 12 pens. Cross over to the "item" side of the diagram, and you can easily see which orders include pens. For systems that physically link objects, the set occurrence diagram is an extremely useful visual tool.

Although the design of the CODASYL network model is very elegant, there were serious problems with implementation. Network databases, much like hierarchical databases, are very diffi-

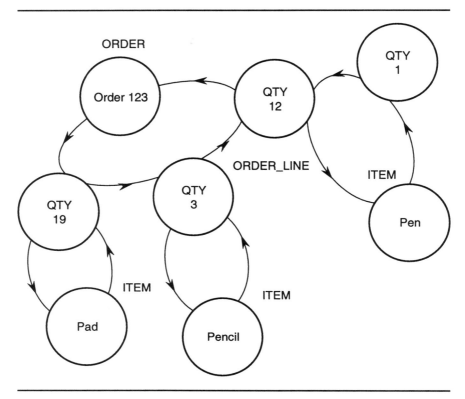

Figure 2.11.   Set occurrence diagram: customer database.

cult to navigate. The Data Manipulation Language (DML), especially for complex navigation, was a skill requiring many months of training.

Structural changes are a nightmare with network databases. Because the data relationships are "hard linked" with embedded pointers, the addition of an index or a new relationship requires special utility programs to "sweep" each and every affected record in the database. As each record is located, the prefix is restructured to accommodate the new pointers. Object-oriented databases encounter this same problem when a class hierarchy requires modification.

CODASYL databases were still far superior to any other technology of the day, and thousands of corporations began to implement their mission-critical systems on IDMS platforms. Even the Air Force used the IDMS database at the North American Air Defense Command (NORAD) to track incoming Soviet missiles (and, of course, Santa Claus at Christmas time). However, as soon as relational databases became fast and stable enough to support mission-critical systems, the cumbersome and inflexible CODASYL systems were abandoned.

Is the CODASYL Network Data Model Returning?

One feature of the object-oriented paradigm is support for recursion. In order to be recursive, a data model must support the ability to reference a record without having to refer to a primary key value. Some researchers have proposed a method for assigning "Object IDs" to identify an object, but relational models cannot address the high overhead and potential problems involved in generating OBJECT IDs. Others have proposed a data model that allows a single field to contain multiple values, or even another table (Kim, 1989). In a procedural language such as C++, the problem of recursion is addressed very elegantly with pointers to structures.

The ODMG standard for object-oriented databases requires unique object IDs to identify each object, and they have deliberately not addressed the ability to access a row based on the data contents of the row.

Many researchers have noted remarkable similarities between the CODASYL Network Model (NWM) and the requirements for object-oriented databases (Schek, 1990). The CODASYL model supports the declaration of abstract "sets" to relate classes together, and CODASYL also supports the notion of "currency," whereby a record may be accessed without any reference to its data attributes. CODASYL databases provide currency tables that allow the programmer to "remember" the most recently accessed record of each type, and the most recently accessed record within a set.

Schek and Scholl (1990) state, "This shows that some of the essential features of the object model can be found in the NWM; NWM records are instances of abstract types manipulated by a limited set of functions (called FINDs), mostly for navigational access. CONNECT and DISCONNECT are used to add or remove objects to or from relationships. Finally, GET retrieves data about the objects into a predefined communications area."

Of all of the existing database models, the CODASYL network model most closely matches the requirements for object-oriented databases, and with some refinement (such as the support of "cyclic" data relationships), the CODASYL model may reemerge in a new form as the standard data model for object-oriented modeling.

Some vendors are already using the CODASYL model as the architecture for object-oriented databases. For example, the C-Data Manager from Database Technologies is an object-oriented database and programming environment based on the CODASYL Network Data Model, and uses ISAM file structures to index its data records.

2.3.4. The Relational Database Model   c. 1980–1990 A.D.

Dr. Ted Codd, a researcher at IBM, developed a model for a "relational" database in which the data resided in "pointerless" tables. These tables could be navigated in a declarative fashion, without the need for any database navigation. Codd called these tables "relations," and relations within his model were very simple to conceptualize and could be viewed as a two-dimensional array of columns and rows. Codd's relational model contained a set of relational "criteria" that must be met for a database to be truly relational. It is interesting that Codd's model of relational characteristics is so stringent that no company has yet offered a commercial database that meets all of his criteria.

Relational databases provide the following improvements over earlier database architectures.

Data independence. The data resides in freestanding tables, which are not hard-linked with other tables. Columns can be added to relational tables without any changes to application programs, and the addition of new data or data relationships to the data model seldom requires restructuring of the tables.

Declarative data access. Database navigation is hidden from the programmers. When compared to a navigational language such as CODASYL DML, in which the programmer is required to know the details of the access paths, relational access is handled with an "SQL" optimizer, which takes care of all navigation on behalf of the user. Relational data access is a "state space" approach, whereby the user specifies the Boolean conditions for the retrieval, and the system returns the data that meets the selection criteria in the SQL statement.

Simple conceptual framework. The relational database is very easy to describe, and even naive users can understand the concept of tables. Complex network diagrams, which are used to describe the structure of network and hierarchical databases, are not needed to describe a relational database.

Referential Integrity (RI). Relational systems allow for the control of business rules with "constraints." These RI rules are used to ensure that one-to-many and many-to-many relationships are enforced within the relational tables. For example, RI would ensure that a row in the CUSTOMER table could not be deleted if orders for that customer exist in the ORDER table.

One of the greatest benefits of the relational databases is the concept of data independence. Because data relationships were no longer hard-linked with pointers, systems developers were able to design systems based on business requirements, with far less time being spent on physical considerations.

Codd's tables, which he termed RELATIONS, consist of columns and rows. Codd chose to call a row a TUPLE (rhymes with "couple"), and he refers to many rows as "instantiations of tuples." Personally, I believe that this obtuse terminology helped to ensure that the relational model gained respect as a legitimate

RI Rule = ORDER.CUST_NAME REFERENCES CUSTOMER.CUST_NAME

Two Options:

ON DELETE RESTRICT   *Customers may not be deleted if they have orders in the ORDER table*

ON DELETE CASCADE   *Customers deletion will cause all orders for the customer to delete.*

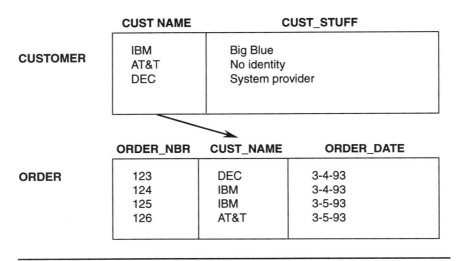

Figure 2.12.   Referential integrity.

offering, and many professionals began to use Codd's confusing terminology.

Codd also introduced the concept of the Structured Query Language (SQL). One should note that SQL is *not* a query language. SQL performs much more than queries (it allows updates, deletes, and inserts), and SQL is also not a language (it is embedded within procedural languages such as COBOL or C). Consequently, the name of Structured Query Language seemed a logical name for Codd's new tool.

SQL offers three classes of operators. The SELECT operator serves to shrink the table vertically by eliminating unwanted rows (tuples). The PROJECT operator serves to shrink the table horizontally, removing unwanted columns, and the JOIN operator allowed the dynamic linking of two tables that share a common column value. Most commercial implementations of SQL do not support a PROJECT operation, and projections are achieved by specifying the columns that are desired in the output. The JOIN operation is achieved by stating the selection criteria for two tables and equating them with their common columns.

The following example incorporates a select, a project, and a join.

```
SELECT CUST_NAME, ORDER_DATE     /*PROJECT columns*/

    FROM CUSTOMER, ORDER

    WHERE

    CUSTOMER.CUST_NBR=ORDER.CUST_NBR  /*JOIN tables*/

    AND CUST_TYPE='NEW'; /*SELECT rows*/
```

The most important feature of the relational database is the ability to isolate the data from the data relationships, and to eliminate the "pointers" that were used by hierarchical and network databases to establish relationships. In a relational database, two tables that have a relationship are defined with a primary key and a foreign key. This key can be used at runtime to dynamically join the tables. Consider the one-to-many relationship between a customer and his or her orders. A relational table declaration would look like this:

```
CREATE TABLE CUSTOMER
(CUST-NO        INTEGER PRIMARY KEY,
 CUST-NAME      CHAR(80),
 CUST-ADDRESS   CHAR(300))

CREATE TABLE ORDER
(ORDER-NO       INTEGER PRIMARY KEY,
 CUST-NO        INTEGER REFERENCES CUSTOMER(CUST-NO) ON
                    DELETE RESTRICT,
```

```
ORDER-DATE     DATE,
ORDER-STUFF    CHAR(80))
```

CUSTOMER TABLE

CUST-#	CUST_NAME	CUST_ADDR
123	Jones, Sam	123 First St.
456	Smyth, Bill	200 Third St
789	Burleson, Don	2100 33rd St.

ORDER TABLE

ORDER-#	CUST-#	ORDER-DATE	ORDER-TYPE
a100	123	3/25/93	prepaid
a101	456	3/26/93	COD
a102	123	3/26/93	COD
a103	789	3/27/93	prepaid

In this model, the "referential integrity" is used to establish the one-to-many relationship and to ensure that no occurrences of the customer record may be deleted if orders exist for that customer. This referential linking method creates tremendous flexibility within the database. The only requirement to join two tables (thereby establishing a one-to-many relationship) is that the fields in the tables share the same type definition. For example, the fields EMP_ID in the EMPLOYEE table and the EMP_NBR field in the SKILL table could be used in a relational join, provided that they have the same data definition (i.e., INTEGER). In a distributed database environment, two tables in completely different systems can be joined at any time, adding to the flexibility of the relational architecture. Object-oriented systems do not support this feature because all data relationships must be rigorously predefined, and ad hoc queries are not supported.

2.3.5. The Object-Oriented Database Model   c. 1990–2000 A.D.

The next progression of database architecture is toward object-oriented databases. Just as early file managers stored data and network databases stored data and relationships, an object-oriented database stores data, data relationships, and the behaviors of the data.

The object-oriented approach borrows heavily from the concepts of "intelligent databases" and "knowledgebases." Both of these approaches advocate storing behaviors within the database such that data and business rules also share a common repository.

With the properties of encapsulation, abstraction, and polymorphism, object technology systems are moving toward a uni-

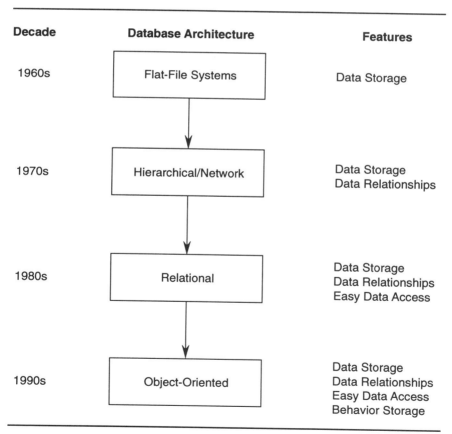

Decade	Database Architecture	Features
1960s	Flat-File Systems	Data Storage
1970s	Hierarchical/Network	Data Storage Data Relationships
1980s	Relational	Data Storage Data Relationships Easy Data Access
1990s	Object-Oriented	Data Storage Data Relationships Easy Data Access Behavior Storage

Figure 2.13.   Evolution of database architectures.

fied data model that models the real world far more effectively than previous modeling techniques. Furthermore, a properly designed object-oriented model promises to be maintenance-free, because all changes to data attributes and behaviors become database tasks and not programming tasks.

Let's take a look at a human analogy to the object-oriented approach. It is very natural for humans to recognize objects, and to associate objects with their classes. It is also a very natural concept to associate an object with its expected behaviors.

Even as very young children we learned to associate behaviors with certain characteristics of objects. For example, it is not uncommon to visit the zoo and hear a three-year-old call all four-legged animals "doggies." The child has learned to associate an object class (dog) with a data attribute (four legs). Later a child will refine his or her object-oriented paradigm and associate other data attributes with animal objects. A child also learns to associate behaviors (i.e., playing, having fun, pain) with different visual and auditory stimuli. Many young children learn to associate unpleasant behaviors (pain) with a visit to the man who wears a white lab coat (the doctor). McDonald's Corporation has spent millions of dollars exploiting this principle, much to the consternation of many parents, associating pleasant behaviors with objects such as golden arches, happy meals, and Ronald McDonald.

Adults develop the same associations between objects and behaviors. There have been hundreds of psychological studies proving that "expectations," or the association of behaviors to attributes, affect interactions between people. When a person enters a doctor's office and sees a person in a white coat, the person is categorized as belonging to object DOCTOR, which implies membership with the class PEOPLE, the subclass EDUCATED PERSON, and the subclass WEALTHY_PERSON. Object classifications will also affect the expected behaviors. For example, waitresses categorize some customers as belonging to the class CHEAPSKATE, and expect small tipping behaviors. An interesting study by Professor Dick Harris of the University of New Mexico is titled "Cheaper by the Bunch," and describes how waitresses categorize large groups of people as being cheaper, expecting these groups to leave a proportionally smaller tip.

Behaviors must be dynamic, and human experience shows

that human associations of behaviors with attributes also change with time. In the 1930s, people with tattoos were usually categorized as belonging to the SAILOR class, whereas today tattoos are indicative of the CRIMINAL class of humans. The ODMG object model partially addressed this issue, whereby objects are assigned lifetimes by the object-oriented database system.

Humans are also familiar with the concept of abstraction. Intangible objects such as time are easily understood, and the conceptual, nonconcrete existence of time has meaning to most individuals.

2.4.   SUMMARY

The distinguishing characteristic of the object-oriented database is its ability to store data behavior, but how is the behavior of the data incorporated into the database? At first glance, this may seem to be a method for moving application code from a program into a database. While it is true that an object-oriented database stores "behaviors," these databases must also have the ability to manage many different objects, each with different data items.

PROBLEMS AND EXERCISES

1. It has been alleged that the trend toward distributed object-oriented database systems may lead to severe problems. Describe how some of today's trends relate to the early flat-file systems, and what may be done to ensure that object-oriented databases do not suffer from the same problems as pre-database systems.

2. The relational database model and the object-oriented model are in total disagreement about several philosophical areas. Describe how the object-oriented principle of encapsulation can be made compatible with the relational concept of data independence.

3. Many people have stated that relational databases are too deeply ingrained in the computer culture to be replaced by object-oriented databases. Why do you agree or disagree with this statement?

4. One of the features of the relational database is its

"pointerless" method of establishing data relationships. The use of foreign keys to establish data relationships provides tremendous flexibility. Conversely, one of the features of object-oriented databases is their use of pointers to establish data relationships, and the great speed that these databases have when compared to relational databases. Comment on the use of pointers within a database, and discuss your opinion regarding the value of pointers to represent data relationships.

5. Some have noted a distinct similarity between the network data model and the object-oriented data model. Describe the features that CODASYL databases share with object-oriented databases, and discuss their differences.

6. Some argue that the object-oriented approach is a very "natural" way of viewing the world, and that the artificial concepts

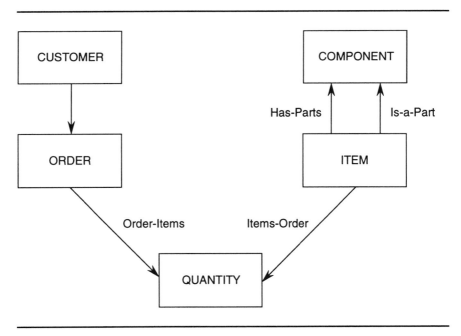

Figure 2.14.   Guttbaum's Hamburgers: entity/relation model.

of tables and rows are a major barrier to future systems development. Describe the relationships between data and objects, and describe how they interact within a database.

7. Using the E/R model for Guttbaum's Hamburgers, state all of the referential integrity rules for this database. Be sure to include all rules that may enforce the data relationships.

8. Use the E/R model for Guttbaum's hamburgers to determine the interaction between the database entities and the following objects:

A. Part-Component Report

Part = Big Meal		
Component	*Component*	*Component*
Hamburger		
	Bun	
	Meat Patty	
		Beef
		Pork
Fries		
Soda		
	Ice	
	Water	
	Flavoring	

B. Customer Order

Date: _____

Customer Name: _____

Address: _____

_____

Order Number: _____

ITEM DESCRIPTION   QUANTITY   PRICE

_____   _____   _____
_____   _____   _____
_____   _____   _____

C. Customer Summary

Report Date: _____

| | Total Number | Total Amount |
Customer Name	of Orders	of All Orders
_____	_____	_____
_____	_____	_____
_____	_____	_____

REFERENCES

Atkinson, D., et al., "The Object-Oriented Database Systems Manifesto," *Deductive and Object-Oriented Databases* (New York: Elsevier Science Publishers, 1990).

Banerjee, J., "Data model issues for object-oriented applications," *ACM Transactions on Office Information Systems,* 5(1):3–26, 1987.

Brathwaite, K., *Object-Oriented Database Design: Concepts and Applications* (San Diego, CA: Academic Press, 1993).

Brown, A.W., *Object-Oriented Databases and Their Applications to Software Engineering* (New York: McGraw-Hill, 1991).

Burleson, D., "SQL generators," *Database Programming & Design,* July 1993.

Cattell, R.G.G., Rogers, T., "Combining object-oriented and relational models of data," International Workshop on Object-Oriented Database Systems, Proceedings, Wash., DC, IEEE Computer Society Press, 1986.

Codd, E.F., *The Relational Model for Database Management,* Version 2 (Reading, MA: Addison-Wesley, 1990).

Date, C.J., *An Introduction to Database Systems* (Reading, MA: Addison-Wesley, 1990).

Dittrich, K., "Object-oriented database systems: the notions and the issues," International Workshop on Object-Oriented Database Systems, Proceedings, Wash., DC, IEEE Computer Society Press, 1986.

Dittrich, K., Dayal, U., Buchmann, P., *On Object-Oriented Database Systems* (New York: Springer-Verlag Publishers, 1991).

Kim, W., *Introduction to Object-Oriented Databases* (Cambridge, MA: The MIT Press, 1990).

Kim, W., "Research directions in object-oriented database systems," *Communications of the ACM,* March 1990.

Loomis, M., "Integrating objects with relational technology," *Object Magazine,* July/August 1991.

Loomis, M., "Object and relational technology. Can they cooperate?," *Object Magazine,* July/August 1991.

Loomis, M., Atwood, T., Cattel, R., Duhi, J., Ferran, G., Wade, D., "The ODMG Object Model," *Journal of Object-Oriented Programming,* June 1993.

McFadden, F., Hoffer, J., *Database Management* (Menlo Park, CA: Benjamin Cummings Publishing Company, 1987).

Meyer, B., *Object-Oriented Software Construction* (New York: Prentice-Hall Publishers, 1988).

Schek, H., Scholl, M., "Evolution of data models," International Workshop on Object-Oriented Database Systems, Proceedings, Wash., DC, IEEE Computer Society Press, 1990.

Yourdon, E., "The marriage of relational and object-oriented design," *Relational Journal,* Vol. 3, Issue 6, Jan. 1992.

3

Object-Oriented Database Development

3.1. INTRODUCTION

Inadequate analysis and planning is one of the foremost reasons that many organizations fail to fully exploit their database systems. Most, if not all, business systems are developed in isolation, and very little energy is spent analyzing the data requirements of the organization as a whole. The focus is on the requirements of the individual systems, with little if any thought about how the system may communicate with other systems in the enterprise. Most organizations are eager to see tangible results, and the database designer does not always have the time to perform a proper data analysis before systems construction begins. In fact, studies have indicated that organizations often ignore database analysis, only to pay a much higher price when their systems require changes. With the advent of "enterprise modeling," there has been a renewed interest in strategic database planning, and many organizations are realizing that the roles of the Database Administrator and Data Administrator are critical for strategic information systems planning.

Unlike traditional database development where a programmer defines and modifies the table structures as needed, object-oriented database development requires a well-defined plan before any database construction may be undertaken.

With object-oriented databases, all of the data attributes and behaviors must be carefully predefined, and consequently, there will be a much longer systems analysis phase than with traditional database development. This is often a problem for organizations that require fast results (i.e., system code) as a benchmark of the progress. Even after repeated lessons on the importance of planning, many companies remain unwilling to invest time in proper planning.

Part of the role of the "enterprise designer" is to define the data requirements of all areas within the organization and to ensure that all data components have well-defined interfaces. With the push toward open system architectures, such as parallel midrange computers, there is an increasing need for this vital function. Without strategic data planning, many companies risk returning to the environments of the 1960s, where each department was governed by "islands of information" and communication between departments was cumbersome.

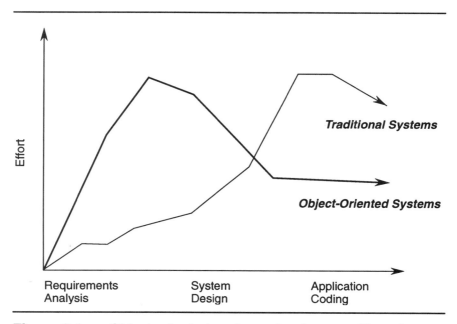

Figure 3.1.   Object-oriented systems development lifecycle.

In order to properly describe the environment of an object-oriented system, the designer needs to be able to develop a conceptual framework. Object-oriented systems view the world at a much higher level than traditional systems, and unlike traditional analysis, it is no longer necessary to de-partition systems down to the data element level. Object-oriented databases view the system components as physical "objects" (i.e., order forms, invoices) rather than as abstract data definitions.

Each individual perceives the real world from the framework of personal experiences, and each individual's conceptual framework determines how he or she looks at the world. Most veterans of data processing are accustomed to viewing databases as being populated with rows, columns, and fields. The object-oriented database analyst must learn to view the world at a higher level, viewing "objects" as consolidations of many columns and rows.

Conceptualization allows a person to look at an object, and the introduction of new concepts to our frame of reference allows us to see new applications for existing objects. This "conceptual

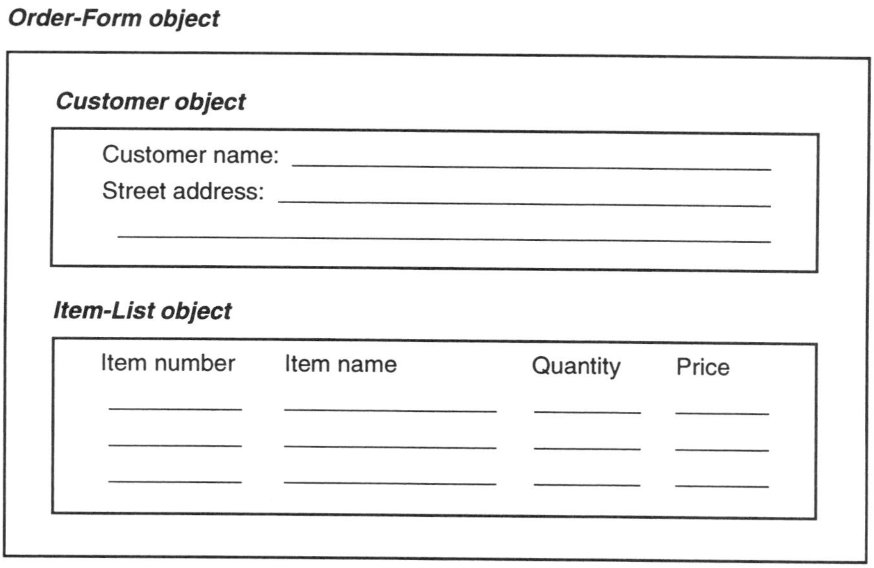

Order-Form object

Customer object

Customer name: _____

Street address: _____

_____

Item-List object

Item number	Item name	Quantity	Price
_____	_____	_____	_____
_____	_____	_____	_____
_____	_____	_____	_____

Figure 3.2.   Objects may be composed of other objects.

reversal" is used by many creative thinkers when they come up with novel uses for existing principles.

Consider Johann Gutenberg, the inventor of the first printing press. Gutenberg combined two unconnected concepts into a new conceptual framework. He noticed that the wine press served to apply force over an area to extract grape juice, and that the purpose of a coin punch was to imprint an image onto a small surface. Gutenberg deduced that a press could be developed that could use pressure to create an imprint over a large surface area.

In fact, most creative inventions come from "breaking the rules" and developing a conceptual framework that did not previously exist. Einstein developed the theory of relativity by imagining an elevator falling at the speed of light, and Alexander Graham Bell developed the telephone from a conceptual model of the human ear.

Concepts allow us to develop recognition about the classification of objects. For example, most people use the concept of "wings" to classify airplanes and the concept of "hull" to identify ships. But what happens when an object such as the Alberta Clipper, the famous seaplane, crosses the conceptual boundaries of two object classes? Sharing characteristics from two concepts, the Alberta Clipper inherits the behaviors and attributes of both aircraft and ships.

Note that concepts are not required to have any physical existence. Object-oriented systems allow for the use of "abstract," or intangible, classes, which do not have any concrete objects.

This idea of conceptualization can be directly applied to object-oriented database analysis. The primary goal of object-oriented database analysis is to identify the behaviors (which may be intangible) and the data (which may be nonquantifiable). If the goal of object-oriented databases is to closely model the real world, both concrete and abstract data as well as behaviors must be accounted for in the database analysis.

Object-oriented analysis (OOA) requires the designer to identify the relevant entities, all relationships between these entities, and a generalization hierarchy that decomposes the entities into subclasses. This involves developing a conceptual framework for the system; the perception of the designer can have a tremendous impact on the final design.

	Behavior	Data
Abstract	Altruism Kindness Cruelty	Morale Level Team Spirit Work Ethic
Concrete	Place an Order Print an Invoice Check Credit Rating	Customer Name Shoe Size Invoice Number

Figure 3.3.   Object-oriented databases must model abstract concepts.

In a traditional systems development project, a *structured specification* is prepared to logically describe the hierarchy of processes, the data flowing between processes, and the functionality of each process. The structured specification document provides a complete identification of the system components from a logical perspective.

Traditional Analysis

Structured Specification:

Data flow diagram (DFD)
Data Dictionary
Process logic specifications (minispecs)

Object-oriented analysis has the goal of delineating the objects, determining the relationships between the objects, and understanding the behaviors of each object. Whereas a traditional analysis is focused is on the transformation of data, object-oriented analysis has a focus on the encapsulation of object behaviors and the interactions between the objects. This method is an extension of traditional analysis techniques and begins with a structured specification.

Object-Oriented Analysis

Start with a traditional structured specification.

List all objects—List the data contents of each *noun*, or physical entity, on the DFD.

List all system behaviors—List all *verbs* within the process names (i.e., *prepare* summary report, *generate* invoices).

Associate the primary behaviors (services) with each object—Each object will have behaviors that uniquely belong to the object. Other objects may request the behavior of the object.

Describe the contracts in the system—A *contract* is an agreement between two objects such that one object will invoke the services of the other.

Create a script for each object—A script describes each initiator, action, participant, and service.

Classify each object and establish object relationships—Generate an entity/relationship model and a generalization hierarchy (ISA) for each object, using traditional E/R or normalization techniques.

3.2.   TRADITIONAL SYSTEMS ANALYSIS

There are three commonly accepted methods for systems analysis: the Gane & Sarson method, the Yourdon method, and the DeMarco systems analysis method. All of these models share a common goal. Before any physical construction of the system may begin, the new systems must be completely analyzed to determine the "functional primitive" processes and the data flows between the processes. This logical specification is used as the input to the systems design. But how does the systems analysis change when an object-oriented database system is being developed?

There is a debate today about whether traditional systems analysis methods are appropriate for object-oriented systems (Martin, 1992). James Martin argues that traditional systems analysis techniques are not appropriate for object-oriented development because the same "object model" is used for analysis, design, and implementation. Therefore, the conceptual walls between analysis, design, and implementation are torn down, and these activities are melded together into a single effort.

However, regardless of the type of system being created, a logical analysis must precede the start of systems design, and the design must be completed before programming may begin. In an effort to consolidate the systems development methodologies, research papers have been published about the proper way to incorporate object-oriented development into existing analysis and design methodologies (Gorman, 1991).

One must always remember that the purpose of systems analysis is to logically identify the processes and the data moving between the processes, and to describe the processing rules and data items. Only after these are defined can design begin, regardless of the physical implementation of the system. While the design strategy may be very different from other systems, object-oriented analysis should begin with the creation of a structured specification. A structured specification is a document that describes all of the data, data storage, external entities, and processes of the system. This document is then used in the design phase for the creation of the behaviors, entity/relation model, and class hierarchy.

3.2.1.   The Structured Specification

1. **Data flow diagrams**—A set of top-down diagrams that depict all processes within the system, the data flows between the processes, and the data stores. The data flow diagrams (DFDs) begin at a very general level and become progressively more

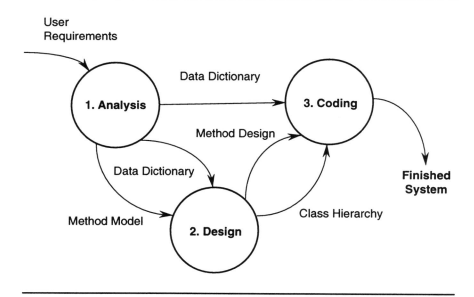

Figure 3.4.   Object-oriented systems development lifecycle.

detailed. The lowest level of processing is called the "functional primitive" level, and this primitive level has been traditionally used as the starting point for systems design.

2. **Data dictionary**—A description of all of the logical data items, including all data flows and data stores (Files).
3. **Process logic specifications (minispecs)**—A description of all functional primitive processes. A process is defined as an operation that modifies a data flow. The tools used to describe processes include pseudocode, procedure flowcharts, decision trees, and decision tables.

Level 1 DFD Process Logic Specification for the PLACE_ORDER Behavior

```
Minispec for PLACE_ORDER:

IF TOTAL_AMT > 1000
    Check CREDIT_RATING in CUSTOMER
```

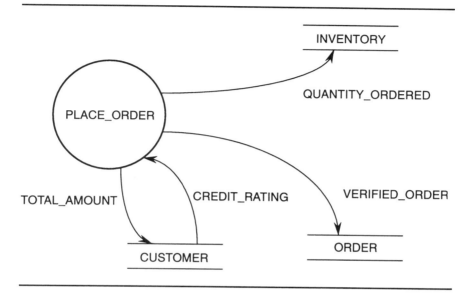

Figure 3.5. Level 1 DFD.

```
    IF CREDIT_RATING = 'BAD' then reject order
        ELSE Store ORDER RECORD
end if

FOR (each item on the order)

    — compare QTY_ORDERED in ORDER with QTY_ON_HAND in ITEM
        IF QTY_ON_HAND < QTY_ORDERED
            Remove item from order
            Prepare backorder slip
        ELSE

    — Add the item to the order
        Subtract QTY_ORDERED from QTY_ON_HAND
        Move QTY_ORDERED to QTY in LINE_ITEM
        Store LINE_ITEM record
NEXT ITEM
```

In a traditional systems analysis, the data dictionary definitions for all data items are "normalized," or grouped, into database entities, which eventually become relational tables. These entities establish the basic entity/relation model for the database engine. Because an object-oriented system incorporates behaviors (messages) into its design, an object-oriented analysis must carefully focus on the interaction between processes and files within the system.

Consider the interaction between the PLACE_ORDER process and the data files. The process PLACE_ORDER uses the data flow TOTAL_AMNT to check the credit rating in the CUSTOMER file. It also uses QTY_ORDERED to check the inventory level for the item, then moves QTY_ORDERED to the LINE_ITEM record, and finally stores this record in the file. The simple process PLACE_ORDER therefore invokes four separate database operations.

The DMLs for PLACE_ORDER are:

DML	RECORD
SELECT	on CUSTOMER
SELECT	on ITEM
UPDATE	on ITEM
INSERT	on LINE_ITEM

3.3.   THE IMPORTANCE OF FUNCTIONAL DECOMPOSITION

The principle of top-down analysis tells us to begin our data flow diagram (DFD) at a very general level. The entire system is viewed as a single process called the "context level" DFD. The DFD is then decomposed, adding levels of detail to the model. The pivotal question becomes: Where does one stop decomposing the processes? Any process that could be identified can probably be subdivided to smaller processes, and it is possible to decompose a DFD to the level where each process represents a single statement. An extreme example of functional decomposition would be showing the statement ADD 1 TO COUNTER as a separate process on the data flow diagram.

Theoreticians tell us that a DFD should be decomposed to the "functional primitive" level (Gane & Sarson, 1976), where each process bubble performs one granular function. Under this definition, one could consider that the PLACE_AN_ORDER behavior performs only one function and is therefore a functional primitive process. With an object-oriented database analysis, especially when it is intended to be used with a relational database, the level of decomposition should correspond to a DML operation so that each behavior operates upon only one object within the system. This allows the use of triggers within a relational database and greatly simplifies the systems design.

The level of partitioning is critical for successful object-oriented systems analysis. For example, the PLACE_ORDER behavior is sufficiently partitioned for a traditional system, where the PLACE_ORDER process would become a program. This program would perform all of the data manipulation, and would therefore have many DML verbs embedded within the code.

For object-oriented relational databases, it is better to continue to decompose the PLACE_ORDER behavior into its subprocesses, namely, CHECK_CREDIT, ADD_ORDER, CHECK_INVENTORY_LEVEL, DECREMENT_INVENTORY, and ADD_LINE_ITEM. These are all subprocesses within the PLACE_ORDER behavior.

```
PLACE_ORDER  (
     CHECK_CREDIT(SELECT on CUSTOMER)
     ADD_ORDER(INSERT on ORDER)
     CHECK_INVENTORY_LEVEL(SELECT on ITEM)
     DECREMENT_INVENTORY(UPDATE on ITEM)
     ADD_LINE_ITEM(INSERT on LINE_ITEM)
               )
```

The behavior PLACE_ORDER is now decomposed into its sub-behaviors.

```
MINISPEC for CHECK_CREDIT

IF TOTAL_AMT > 1000
   Check CREDIT_RATING in CUSTOMER
   IF CREDIT_RATING = 'BAD' then reject order
      ELSE Store ORDER RECORD
end if
```

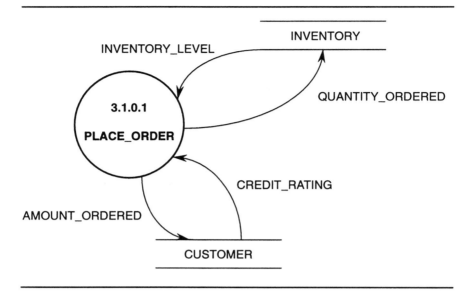

Figure 3.6.   Level 1 DFD.

MINISPEC for CHECK_INVENTORY

FOR (each item on the order)

    — compare QTY_ORDERED in ORDER with QTY_ON_HAND in
ITEM
        IF QTY_ON_HAND < QTY_ORDERED
            Remove item from order
            Prepare backorder slip
NEXT ITEM

MINISPEC for ADD_LINE_ITEM

FOR (each item on the order which is in stock)

    — Add the item to the order
      Subtract QTY_ORDERED from QTY_ON_HAND.

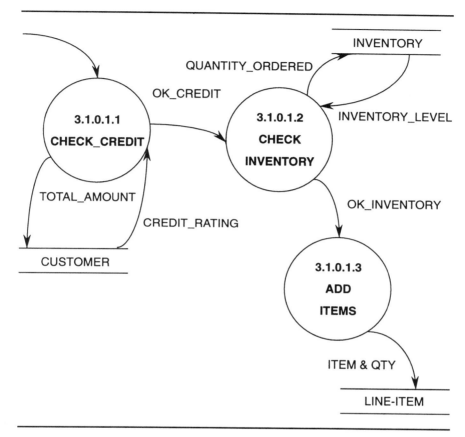

Figure 3.7. Level 2 DFD.

```
Move QTY_ORDERED to QTY in LINE_ITEM.
Store LINE_ITEM record.
```

NEXT ITEM

As you can see, each behavior within the database now corresponds with a single database update operation. The insert on the LINE_ITEM record is associated with the ADD_ITEM behavior. This one-to-one partitioning is only important for database updates, as select operations may still access many records within the database.

There is still a great deal of controversy about the best way to approach database design for object-oriented systems. Architecturally, some theoreticians state that the relational model is not well-suited for use in an object-oriented environment. Others maintain that relational architectures are more suitable for traditional data processing.

It is important to recognize that many object-oriented systems do not exploit many of the features of "classical" database management. To these systems, the only purpose of an OODBMS is to provide "object persistence"; very little weight is given to concurrency-control, roll-back and recovery, and the other features associated with classical databases.

One very important point: An existing database does not have to support all of the formal constructs of the object-oriented approach to benefit from the object-oriented method. For example, object-oriented programming languages allow for the creation of abstract data types. The data types offered in commercial database systems—CHAR INTEGER NUMBER, VARCHAR, BIT—are sufficient for 99.9% of database applications. Some commercial relations database vendors have stated that they will incorporate a user-defined data type in their future releases. Oracle, the popular relational database for midrange computers, has announced that Oracle Version 8 will support abstract data typing.

Some argue that a database must be able to have data types that are lists rather than finite values, and some databases such as UniSQL allow for single data types (fields) to contain lists of values or even another table.

One must remember that the main difference between object-oriented and traditional systems is the idea that both data and behavior are stored in the DBMS. In an object-oriented database, instances of a class may behave differently depending on the processing circumstances. Consider a simple example of how an object-oriented database may differ from traditional systems.

In a traditional database system, all instances of an order record would share the same data items and processing characteristics. Under object-oriented databases, an order will contain not only the order record itself but also the relevant behaviors that are associated with the order. For example, there may be "rush" orders that exhibit behaviors different from a "COD" order.

3.3.1. Object Behavior Analysis

One of the basic distinctions between traditional systems and object-oriented systems is the initiator for the processes. Object-oriented systems are event-driven, unlike traditional systems where a process is triggered by the change to a data item. But how does an analyst shift from thinking about systems in the traditional way to thinking about systems as a collection of interacting objects?

Object behavior analysis is a new method (Rubin, 1992) and contains the following steps:

1. Identify a hierarchy of behaviors for the entire system.
2. Identify the "primitive" behaviors, and create a behavior hierarchy.
3. Identify all objects that exhibit the behaviors, and create a class hierarchy.
4. Associate each primitive behavior with each object class.

The first step is to be able to identify the objects. When isolating the physical objects within the structured analysis document, it is tempting to focus on the nouns within the diagram, and assume that all "things" that represent physical objects should be modeled as objects. While this is true, this approach often ignores the intangible objects, which have a tremendous bearing on the system.

The best approach to understanding a system in object-oriented terms is to change the focus from data flows to object behaviors. Behaviors are events generally associated with verbs, such as "Create Order Form" or "Print Service Request." To properly identify all of the behaviors within a system, it is necessary to take a very top-down approach to system behavior. At a highest level, the overall system can be said to have a behavior, although it is often quite difficult to give the system a meaningful behavior name. Often, entire systems can be labeled with names like "Process Inventory" or "Manage Personnel Records," but it is critical to the development of the object-oriented system to clearly identify each component of the system within a behavioral context.

3.4. TOP-DOWN SYSTEMS ANALYSIS METHODOLOGY

There has always been a misunderstanding about the difference between top-down and bottom-up analysis, especially as it applies to database design. Many database designers who publicly advocate the top-down approach continue to develop systems from a bottom-up standpoint. An excellent analogy is a child who wants to build a tree house and immediately begins nailing boards together. When asked about a plan, he replies that the plan will be much easier to write after he sees the finished product. Database designers fall into the same trap when they focus on the details of a single module and do not consider the scope, or "big picture," of the entire system. This design myopia can lead to database systems that do not communicate properly with other systems; for object-oriented databases, a bottom-up analysis will lead to disaster.

The top-down approach to system development is foreign to many because most scientists are taught the bottom-up approach to problem solving. A statistician, for example, is taught to sample specific data from a population to infer the general state of the population. A physician is taught to look for specific symptoms, which leads to a general diagnosis of a disease.

> Top-Down Analysis
> > General to specific
> > Global to detailed
> Bottom-Up Analysis
> > Specific to general
> > Detailed to global

3.5. AN OBJECT-ORIENTED SYSTEMS ANALYSIS METHODOLOGY

Just as the object-oriented languages are extensions to existing programming languages, object-oriented database analysis is an extension of existing data analysis techniques. As we know, traditional information systems are *data-driven*, in that the requirements of the data determine the sequence of events within the system. Object-oriented systems are *event-driven,* which means that requests for behaviors (also called *services*) determine the sequence of processing within the database.

There are dozens of methods for performing object-oriented analysis, and there is practically no consensus about the "proper" way to model an object-oriented database. It appears that there are many common elements to the different methods, and this text provides a general method for object-oriented analysis.

Object-oriented database analysis differs from traditional analysis because the type of object-oriented implementation will have a direct impact on the analysis. For example, an object-oriented database to be written entirely in C++ will be quite different from an analysis to be implemented with an existing commercial relational database.

STEP 1. Start with a traditional structured specification. A systems analysis document should provide a complete description of the logical system, regardless of the design and implementation of the system. For example, a relational/object-oriented design is going to be very different from a pure object-oriented system that is implemented in C++. A properly prepared data flow diagram will clearly indicate the "objects" to be used for object-oriented design.

STEP 2. Identify and list all objects in the DFD. A review of the data dictionary should indicate which data items are to be modeled as objects. The easiest method is to look for *nouns*, such as "reports" or "documents." These will become the physical objects to be manipulated by the object-oriented database.

Object Listing

OBJECT NAME
Customer Order Form
Item List
Inventory List
Backorder Report
Item Component Report
Customer Enrollment Form

STEP 3. List all system behaviors. To determine the system behaviors, we review the *verbs* within the process names. For example, *"Prepare* summary report" and *"generate* invoices" are process names that indicate events within the system.

Behavior Listing

BEHAVIOR NAME
Prepare invoice
Check customer credit
Check inventory level
Place order
Enroll new customer
Prepare item component listing
Add line items
Prepare backorder listing
Generate warehouse request

STEP 4. List the behaviors provided by each object. An object may have many *behaviors* (services), and each behavior is unique to each object. This does not mean that other objects may not use the behaviors; it only means that the object is the primary owner of the behaviors. Other objects may establish *contracts* with the object in order to use the behavior.

Object/Behavior Cross-Reference List

OBJECT NAME	BEHAVIOR NAME	BEHAVIOR NAME	BEHAVIOR NAME
Customer Order	Enroll customer	Place order	
Item	Add item	Add line item	Create item report
Item List	Place order	Add line item	
Inventory List	Create inventory list		

Backorder Report	Create backorder report	
Item Components	Create component report	
Customer Enrollment	Add customer	Check credit

STEP 5. Describe the contracts in the system. A *contract* is an agreement between two objects such that one object will invoke the services of the other. Because of contracts, a behavior may be called by many objects, and an object may participate in many behaviors. Because there is a many-to-many relationship between objects and behaviors, the association listing should complete the cross-referencing of behaviors and objects.

Behavior/Object Cross-Reference List

BEHAVIOR NAME	OBJECT	OBJECT	OBJECT
Customer order	Customer	Order	Item
Enroll customer	Customer		
Add item	Item		
Add line item	Order		
Create item report			
Place order	Customer	Order	Inventory
Create inventory list	Item	Item Component	
Create backorder report	Item	Order	
Create component report	Item	Component	
Add customer	Customer		
Check credit	Customer		

STEP 6. Create a script for each object. A *script* describes each initiator, participant, and behavior for each object. This describes the interface between all objects and determines how the objects will communicate with each other. For example,

the check-credit behavior would be initiated by passing the data item TOTAL_ORDER_AMOUNT. The action would be to compare TOTAL_ORDER_AMOUNT with the TOTAL_ CREDIT data item in the customer object.

Script Listing

INITIATING BEHAVIOR	PARTICIPANT	BEHAVIOR
Place order	customer	check-credit
Place order	item	check-inventory level

STEP 7. Classify each object and establish object relationships. The final step is to generate an entity/relationship model and a generalization hierarchy (ISA) for the system. All of the lowest-level objects within the script listing will correspond to entities within the database. The following section of this text will fully describe the process of creating entity/relationship models and class hierarchies for each entity.

3.6. OBJECT-ORIENTED DATABASE DESIGN

The goal of object-oriented design is to incorporate the behaviors and data together into a single database system. In an interpretive environment (i.e., FoxPro, dBASE), where the code is parsed and executed at runtime, the source code could reside as a row in a database table and be called at runtime to exhibit the desired behaviors. Or, in a compiled environment such as IDMS, pointers to executable routines could be stored in each instance of a record. The pointer would link the record to a precompiled behavior that would act upon the record.

Another problem is the fact that different objects, although being of the same class, may not contain the same data items. This concept can be incorporated into a CODASYL network database by taking advantage of multimembered sets, or it could be used in a relational architecture by defining all potential data attributes in a class and using the VARCHAR data type with the NULL value clause to compress unused values.

Multimembered "sets" allow different record types to be linked into the same logical relationship. For example, tests scored for the GED, ACT, and SAT could all be lumped together into a single TEST_SCORES relationship, even though each of the test records has very distinct data items.

Another approach is to create a one-of-a-kind (OOAK) base table for the class type, and to establish a one-to-many relationship to subordinate tables, one for each object type within that class. This approach will be fully described in the chapter on designing dynamic class hierarchies (Chapter 5).

Since Professor Peter Chen first published his method for describing the relationships between database entities, there has been a great deal of interest in the formal representation of databases. As a conceptual tool, Chen diagrams (also called E/R models) have become a standard for database design. Unfortunately, many database designers have only a cursory knowledge of the method behind the representation of the database structures, and

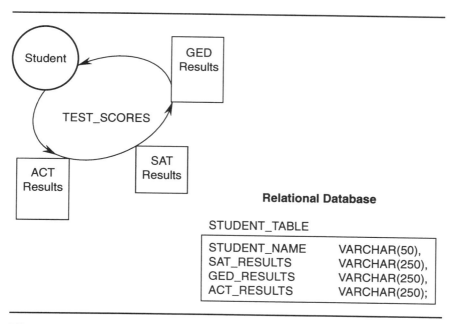

Figure 3.8. Multimembered sets.

this chapter will serve as a step-by-step guide for doing E/R modeling for object-oriented databases.

E/R modeling began shortly after the general availability of the IMS database when it first became understood that a database was required to store more than just data; it had to store information about the relationships between the data items. Researchers such as Ted Codd and Peter Chen began working to describe formal procedures for the representation of data relationships.

Today, E/R modeling is about to take on another dimension of object-oriented data modeling. Object-oriented database systems are required to describe these things:

1. The class hierarchy (DDL)
2. The relationships between the class items (Chen diagrams)
3. The objects within the classes
4. The behaviors of the data items

Unfortunately, many database designers have never been instructed in the similarities between normalization and E/R modeling. As with any database design tool, there is much more to a method than learning the shapes of the diagram icons, just as there is more to playing chess than simply recognizing the pieces and the movement of the pieces.

3.7.   NORMALIZATION OF OBJECT-ORIENTED DATABASES

Let's take a look at the goals of normalization:

1. To control data redundancy
2. To infer relationships between data items
3. To develop a cohesive class hierarchy

GOAL 1. The control of data redundancy. In a hierarchical or CODASYL database, it is possible to define and implement a database system that contains absolutely no redundant information. This is called Third Normal Form, or 3NF. Hierarchical and network databases may be truly free of redundancy because all data relationships are represented through pointers. Because object-oriented systems use pointers to establish data relationships, many object-oriented systems may be designed to be completely free of redundant information. Remember, an absolute elimination of redundancy requires embedded pointers to establish the data relationships, and therefore no relational database can ever be totally free of redundant data.

Any relational database that has one-to-many or many-to-many relationships will have redundant "foreign keys" embedded in the tables to establish the logical relationships. Data relationships are created by the redundant duplication of foreign keys in the subordinate tables in order to make it possible to join the tables together, thereby relating the contents of the data items in these tables.

As the size of the database increases, redundancy becomes a major problem. Today, many users are creating very large databases (VLDBs), many of which contain trillions of bytes. For databases of this size, the introduction of a single byte of additional storage to a row can costs thousands of dollars in additional disk expense. Data redundancy is detrimental for two reasons. Foremost, storage is wasted by duplicating the redundant material. The second and most ominous detriment is the extra processing required when the redundant data items are updated. Very large and highly volatile data items that are redundantly duplicated can cause huge processing bottlenecks.

However, this does not mean to imply that redundancy is always undesirable. Performance is still an overriding factor in most systems, and proper control of redundant information implies that redundant information may be introduced into any structure so long as the performance improvements outweigh the additional disk costs and update problems.

GOAL 2. To infer the relationships between the data items. There are five types of data relationships which must be considered when designing an object-oriented database:

1. One-to-one relationship
2. One-to-many relationship
3. Many-to-many relationship
4. Recursive many-to-many relationship
5. The ISA relationship

One to One (1 to 1) In database modeling, a data item that has a one-to-one relationship with the primary key becomes an attribute of the table. In other words, a data item, say a Social Security number, has a one-to-one relationship with full_name in the PERSON entity; then the Social Security number becomes an attribute of the PERSON entity.

One to many (1 to M) One-to-many relationships imply that a single occurrence of the owner entity may have several occurrences of the subordinate entity, but each subordinate entity will have only one owner.

Father to Son	One father may have many sons; a son has only one father.
Customer to Order	Customers may place many orders; an order is for only one customer.

Many to Many (M to M) The many-to-many relationship implies that an entity has many of the other entity, and a converse relationships exists at the other entity.

Order to Item	Each order "has" many items, and an item "participates" in many orders.

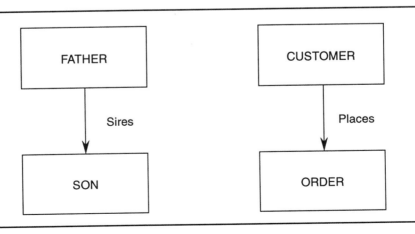

Figure 3.9.   One-to-many relationships.

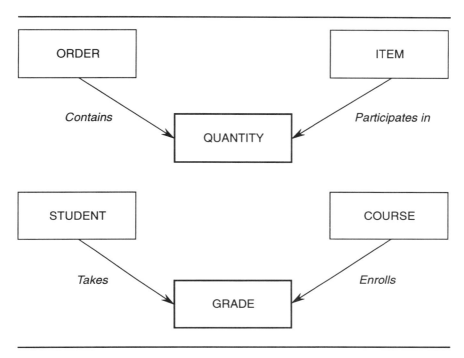

Figure 3.10. Many-to-many relationships.

Student to Classes   A student "takes" many classes, and a class "has" many students.

Note the introduction of the "junction," or intersection table, in these relationships. The junction entity is required to create the many-to-many relationship between the data items. For relational implementations, junction entities must contain the primary keys of their owner entities. Object-oriented databases do not have this requirement, but the junction entities may contain additional data, such as GRADE or QUANTITY_ORDERED.

3.7.1.   Recursive Many-to-Many Relationships

Recursive many-to-many relationships are conditions in which an object has a many-to-many relationship with other occurrences of the same object class. These relationships are sometime called bill-of-materials (BOM) relationships, and the graphical representation of the recursive relationship is sometimes called a bill-of-materials explosion. These relationships are called recursive because a single query may make many sub-passes through the tables to arrive at the solution.

Bill-of-materials relationships describe a condition where an object has a many-to-many relationship with another object within the same class. For example, a part may consist of other parts, and at the same time be a component in a larger assembly. A class at a university may have many prerequisites, and at the same time be a prerequisite for another class. In the legal arena, a court case may cite other cases, and in turn be cited by later cases.

For example, a bill-of-material request for components of a big meal would show that a big meal consists of a hamburger, fries and a coke; a hamburger consists of a meat patty, a bun and a pickle; and a meat patty consists of meat and filler; and so on. Please see the next chapter for a complete discussion of recursive relationships.

3.7.2. A Pragmatic Approach to the Design of Object Class Hierarchies

In the world of mathematics, it has been shown that farmers often demonstrate a knowledge of applied calculus without ever having taken a class in calculus. This phenomenon has been called "barnyard" calculus, and demonstrates the point that many advanced

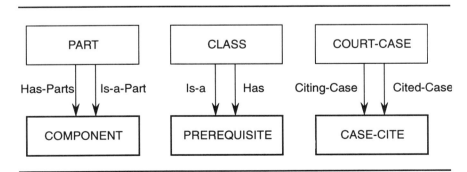

Figure 3.11. Recursive many-to-many relationships.

theoretical constructs can be applied without formal education or background. In database design, it is often true that many database designers apply "common sense" knowledge of E/R modeling without having any formal education. After all, data normalization is nothing more than a formal restatement of common sense principles, and one does not require an advanced degree in database design to know that similar data items should be placed together in a relational table.

The formal rules of normalization according to Dr. Codd are very formal and rigorous:

> **First Normal Form (1NF)**—A relation is in first normal form if it contains no repeating data items.
>
> **Second Normal Form (2NF)**—A relation is in second normal form if and only if it is in first normal form and each no-key attribute is fully functionally dependent on the entire concatenated key.
>
> *or*
>
> A relation is in second normal form if each attribute depends on the key, the whole key, and nothing but the key, so help me Codd!
>
> **Third Normal Form (3NF)**—A relation is in third normal form if and only if it is in second normal form and there are no transitive dependencies between no-key data items.

Other theoreticians, who were anxious to apply mathematical rigor to database design, created additional cases of form normalization, including Boyce-Codd Normal Form, Fourth Normal Form, and Fifth Normal Form. These are very special cases of data relationships that are usually of little interest to the practicing database designer.

Regardless of the normalization and design theory, there is still the haunting question about the proper data structure suitable for an object-oriented database. Most practicing systems developers follow a set of common sense rules for designing their systems, and they will usually arrive at the same conclusions as those who formally normalize their data. The common sense approach generally includes the following step:

Determine the entities. Without resorting to the rigorous definitions imposed by Dr. Codd, a database can simply be stated as: "What data items belong together?"

When grouping like items together, it is obvious that a student's address belongs in the STUDENT entity and that a room number belongs with a BUILDING entity, but certain questions arise when one attempts to determine the level of partitioning for the entities.

For example, assume that you have been asked to design a database for a university. The university has provided you with the following list of data items:

  student name
  course number
  semester
  room number
  building name
  instructor name
  student street address
  student zip code
  student hair color

Given this simple example, it is very easy to group like data items together and establish the relationships. However, this is only the first step in object-oriented database design.

3.8   MISLEADING MANY-TO-MANY RELATIONSHIPS

Consider the association of the HAIR_COLOR attribute to the STUDENT entity. Is there is a many-to-many between hair color and student? After all, there are many students with blonde hair, and blonde hair is possessed by many students. Why, then, would we not create a many-to-many relationship between STUDENT and HAIR_COLOR? The solution depends on whether there are other nonkey data items within the HAIR_COLOR entity.

If there were many data items relating to hair color, it would be perfectly appropriate to create another entity called

Misleading Data Relationships

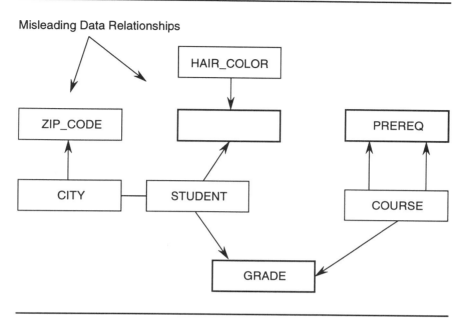

Figure 3.12.   Misleading data relationships.

HAIR_COLOR. But in this case, even though a many-to-many relationship exists between HAIR_COLOR and STUDENT, HAIR_COLOR is a standalone data attribute, and it would not be necessary to create an additional data structure.

Consider the attribute ZIP_CODE in the STUDENT entity. Is there a violation of third normal form (i.e., a transitive dependency) between STUDENT-CITY and ZIP_CODE? In other words, it appears that if a ZIP_CODE is known for a student, then they also know the city where they reside. This makes sense, and it therefore follows that there is a one-to-many relationship between ZIP_CODE and CITY, such that one CITY may have many ZIP_CODE, but a ZIP_CODE is only for one city. The presence of this data relationship makes it tempting to create a separate entity called ZIP, which has student entities attached to it. However, here again is another case where the lack of no-key attributes for the ZIP entity makes it impractical to create the

ZIP entry. In other words, ZIP_CODE does not have any associated data items, and it does not make sense to create a database table with only one data field.

This example demonstrates that it is not enough to group "like" items together and then identify the data relationships. A practical test must be made regarding the presence of no-key attributes within an entity class. If an entity does not have any attributes (i.e., there is only one field in the table), then the presence of the entity is nothing more than an index to the foreign key in the member entity, and should be removed from the E/R model.

3.9.   INTRODUCING REDUNDANCY FOR PERFORMANCE

Codd's rules of normalization, with their emphasis on removing data redundancy, makes many database designers feel that all data redundancy is undesirable, and that the goal of normalization and E/R modeling is to remove all data redundancy. Actually, the goal is to control redundancy and not to remove

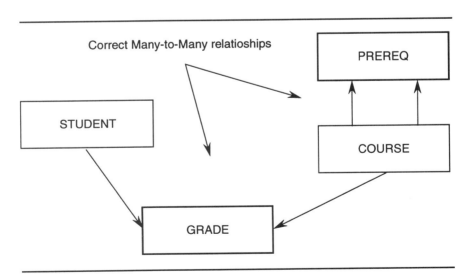

Figure 3.13.   Correct many-to-many relationships.

redundancy. Clearly, a database with widespread redundancy is wasteful, but the question becomes moot if there are no clear rules about reintroducing redundancy into the system to increase performance.

There are many situations where a database in third normal form (3NF) is inappropriate for a production system. Once upon a time, a naive database designer created a student registration database for a major university and designed the database "according to Codd," with absolutely no data redundancy. The system worked fine in testing, but when it came time to register the 20,000 students who were enrolled at the university, the database performed miserably, and students were forced to wait for hours to get registered for classes. An emergency database design team was flown in to redesign the crippled database, and the addition of redundant data increased the performance to acceptable levels.

While the elimination of redundancy is an excellent goal, it is of little importance if your response time is measured in minutes rather than seconds. Only by carefully introducing redundancy into the database design can acceptable performance be achieved.

The introduction of redundancy into a database is essentially a cost/benefit analysis. There are two types of costs that must always be considered when a redundant data item is introduced into your model:

1. What is the "cost" for the redundant item (in terms of disk space)?
2. What is the processing cost for updating the redundant item in two places?

There are two issues: the size of the data item and the volatility of the data item. A very small and stable data item would not be a problem to introduce redundantly into a system. Consider a field EMPLOYEE-SEX. This field is only one byte and, barring a trip to Sweden, EMPLOYEE-SEX will never change in value. Therefore, this item would be a far more acceptable redundant item than would a field like CURRENT-ADDRESS, which consumes many bytes and requires frequent updating.

3.10.   THE "ISA" RELATIONSHIP

After establishing a class hierarchy with the entity/relation model, the principle of generalization is used to identity the class hierarchy and the level of abstraction associated with each class. Generalization implies a successive refinement of the class, allowing the superclasses of objects to inherit the data attributes and behaviors that apply to the lower levels of the class. Generalization establishes "taxonomy hierarchies," which organize the classes according to their characteristics, usually in increasing levels of detail. Generalization begins at a very general level and proceeds to a specific level, with each sublevel having its own unique data attributes and behaviors.

In the figure below, the ISA relationship is used to create a hierarchy within the object class, and all of the lower-level classes will inherit the behaviors. The ISA relationship is used to

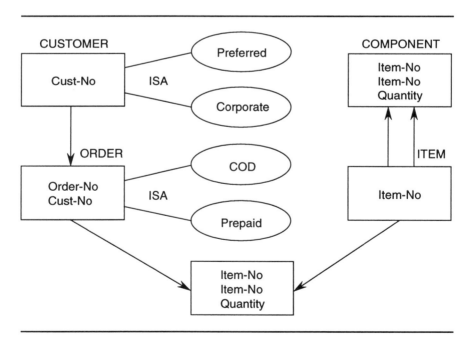

Figure 3.14.   E/R model with ISA relationships.

model the hierarchy that is created as the class entity is decomposed into its logical subcomponents. Customers may be PREFERRED_CUSTOMERS or NEW_CUSTOMERS, and orders may be COD_ORDERS or PREPAID_ORDERS, each with their own data items and behaviors.

Let's look at an application of this system for a vehicle dealership. Occurrences of ITEMs to a dealership are VEHICLEs, and beneath the vehicle class, we may find subclasses for cars and for boats. Within cars, the classes may be further partitioned into classes for TRUCK, VAN, and SEDAN. The VEHICLE class would contain the data items that are unique to vehicles, including the vehicle ID and the year of manufacture. The CAR class, because it ISA VEHICLE, would inherit the data items of the VEHICLE class. The CAR class might contains data items such as the num-

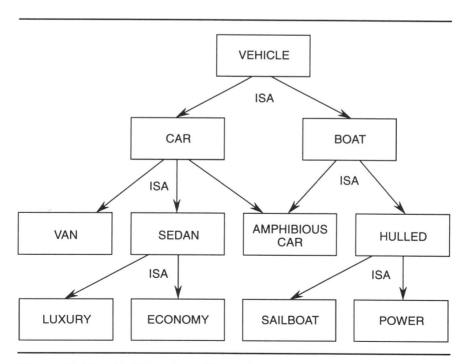

Figure 3.15.   Vehicle class hierarchy.

ber of axles and the gross weight of the vehicle. Because the VAN class ISA CAR, which in turn ISA VEHICLE, objects of the VAN class will inherit all data items and behaviors relating to CARS and VEHICLES.

Not all classes within a generalization hierarchy will have objects associated with them. The object-oriented paradigm allows for abstraction, which means that a class may exist only for the purpose of passing inherited data and behaviors. The classes VEHICLE and CAR would probably not have any concrete objects, while objects within the VAN class would inherit from the abstract VEHICLE and CAR classes.

Multiple inheritance is also demonstrated by the AMPHIBIOUS_CAR class. Any instances of this class will inherit data and behaviors from both the CAR and the BOAT classes.

It is important to note that there is a very big difference between one-to-many relationships and ISA relationships. The ISA construct does not imply any type of recurring association, while the one-to-many and many-to-many relationships imply multiple occurrences of the subclasses. In the above example, this entire class hierarchy describes vehicles that are associated with the ITEM entity in the overall database, and class hierarchies *do not* imply data relationships between the classes. While one CUSTOMER may place many ORDERS, it is not true that one CAR may have many SEDANS.

3.11. THE OBJECT-ORIENTED ENTITY/ RELATIONSHIP MODEL (OOERM)

A recent publication outlines a method for designing object-oriented entity/relation models (Gorman, 1991). Gorman describes a model called OOERM, which alleges to provide a method for describing object-oriented data models with entity/relation diagram tools. While this model does a very good job at modeling the behaviors of the data, the model ignores the individual objects that constitute each class.

However, the OOERM model is very useful for adding formalism and describing a procedure for describing behaviors and message interaction between behaviors (McFadden, 1991). McFadden elaborates on the concepts of messages (parameters) that are passed between behaviors in an object-oriented database, but he confuses OBJECTS and CLASSES within the OOERM Model. As we know, the rectangle in the E/R model represents a CLASS, or a collection of related OBJECTS. Properly stated, a reference to a behavior within the database would need to include

1. The object to be manipulated (i.e., COD_ORDER)
2. The name of the behavior (i.e., PLACE_ORDER)
3. Any messages passed between the object and the behavior

such that a call to the behavior might look like

```
PLACE_ORDER(COD_ORDER())
```

Because behaviors must allow for the inheritance of the behaviors of their superclasses, a PLACE_ORDER behavior would need to include its sub-behaviors, CHECK_CREDIT and CHECK_INVENTORY. CHECK_INVENTORY may also have the sub-behaviors ADJUST_INVENTORY and ADD_LINE_ITEM, such that a call to PLACE_ORDER is really expanded to

```
PLACE_ORDER(COD_ORDER(

    CHECK_CREDIT(PREFERRED_CUSTOMER)

    CHECK_INVENTORY(

        ADJUST_INVENTORY(UPDATE ITEM)

        ADD_LINE_ITEM(INSERT ORDER_LINE)

            )

    )
```

In the OOERM model, the entities and relationships are identical to the entities and relationships in a conventional E/R model, but oval-shaped symbols have been added to describe the behaviors associated with the model. It is very easy to get an OOERM diagram that quickly becomes unreadable, especially when there are many behaviors associated with the database. Also, the OOERM model does not even address the nesting of behaviors.

Figure 3.16 shows how an OOERM would appear for Guttbaum's hamburger stand. Note that the behaviors are added as ovals, with the arrows representing the data that is passed to the behaviors.

Consider the behavior PLACE_ORDER. This behavior has other behaviors nested within it, and ADD_ITEMS and CHECK_CREDIT must both successfully complete before PLACE_ORDER may execute. Notice that ITEM_LIST is passed to the ADD_ITEMS behavior, which then interrogates the ITEM

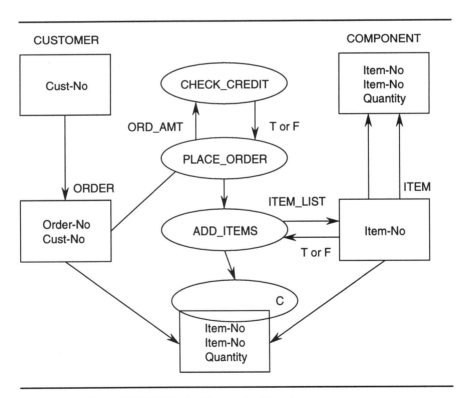

Figure 3.16.   OOERM: Guttbaum's Hamburgers.

record to see if the requested item is in stock. The boolean "True or False" is passed back to ITEM_LIST for each item in the order. For each item in stock, the ADD_ITEM behavior will then decrement the inventory in the ITEM record (by issuing an UPDATE command), and then add new rows to the LINE ITEM table, one for each item requested. Gorman uses a subset of relational behaviors to indicate alteration of data items in the database. The superimposed oval over the LINE_ITEM table, indicates a DML operation (INSERT, UPDATE, DELETE) on the table, with the "C" indicating a CREATE operation. Create operations are used to describe the creation of a new object class, while Add operations are used to describe the addition of a object within a class. The OOERM model would indicate a delete with a "D."

While OOERM is a very useful diagramming technique for describing the behaviors of an object-oriented database, it has two major drawbacks. The first is the failure of the model to describe the objects within each class. For example, the ORDER class has two object types, COD_ORDER and PREPAID_ORDER, both of which have different behaviors. The OOERM diagram as shown in Figure 3.16 would be misleading in the case of a PREPAID_ORDER, which would not require a CREDIT_CHECK behavior.

The second major drawback of the OOERM model is the failure of the model to associate behaviors directly with database DML operations such as INSERT, UPDATE or DELETE. In this example, the INSERT behavior of the LINE_ITEM tables is always associated with the ADD_ITEM behavior. Nonupdate statements (i.e., SQL SELECT) would also be useful to show in such a diagram. For example, the CREDIT_CHECK behavior is always associated with an SQL SELECT of the CUSTOMER table. UPDATE operations also present a dilemma. An ADJUST_INVENTORY behavior would serve to UPDATE the ITEM table, but a CHANGE_ITEM_DESCRIPTION would also UPDATE the ITEM record.

Because a single SQL UPDATE may be associated with several behaviors, a method needs to be devised that will show the connection between behaviors and DML. For example, the OOERM clearly shows the PLACE_AN_ORDER behavior, but it does not show the different processing that occurs for permutations of the behavior. PLACE_ORDER(COD_ORDER)) is going to have different interactions than will PLACE_ORDER (PREPAID_ORDER)), and it becomes very difficult to graphically depict the differences in the behavior.

In conclusion, the OOERM method is very useful for describing the behaviors of the data within the database, and showing the interaction of the behaviors with data items, but it does not describe the differences between the behaviors as they act upon different object of the same class. This is not meant as a condemnation of the OOERM method, because there is no two-dimensional diagramming tool that can clearly describe the third and fourth dimensions required for object-oriented modeling.

Bernhard Thalheim identified several problems with Professor Chen's entity/relation model and the application to object-oriented entity/relation modeling. He developed a similar model that he dubbed HERM (High-Order Entity/Relation Model). The HERM model is based on the premise that traditional E/R techniques can only model first-order relationships and the fact that ISA relationships cannot be modeled naturally (Thalheim, 1990).

3.12. A BETTER ENTITY/RELATIONSHIP MODEL

If a proper database design has been performed, the addition of objects to the entity/relation model is very straightforward. Existing principles for database design do not change when designing an object-oriented database; it simply takes a new dimension as each entity is partitioned into objects. An object-oriented database design must begin with a normalized set of relations in third normal form.

In object-oriented databases, each instance of an entity corresponds to a "class" within the object-oriented paradigm. Contrary to popular belief, a "class hierarchy" is not a hierarchy at all, in the sense that it is composed of descending one-to-many relationships.

A class hierarchy may contain implied many-to-many relationships, such as the ORDER-ITEM relationship, as well as recursive many-to-many relationships, as is the case with the PART-COMPONENT relationship. In the case of the ORDER-ITEM relationship, we are representing the fact that an order may contain many items, and that an item may participate in many orders. The PART-COMPONENT recognizes that different occurrences of the PART class may have many-to-many relationships with other parts. For example, a cheeseburger has many parts (i.e., 2 bun halves, 1 patty), and at the same time may be a part of a larger part, such as a big meal.

There are two ways to graphically illustrate data relationships: one uses relational tables and the other uses linked-lists. Both methods link the information together, but they perform the function in very different ways.

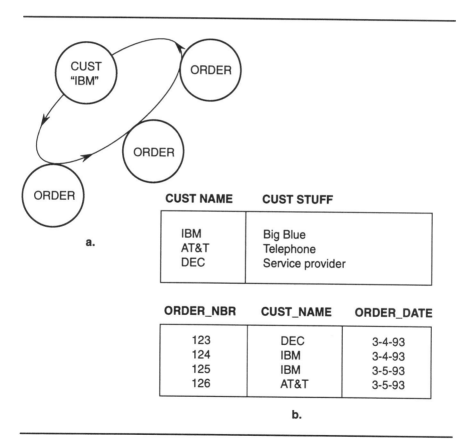

a.

CUST NAME	CUST STUFF
IBM	Big Blue
AT&T	Telephone
DEC	Service provider

ORDER_NBR	CUST_NAME	ORDER_DATE
123	DEC	3-4-93
124	IBM	3-4-93
125	IBM	3-5-93
126	AT&T	3-5-93

b.

Figure 3.17.   a. Linked-list relationships; b. foreign-key relationships.

Now that our classes are identified, where do we go from here? We know that an object is defined as an instance of a class, and common sense tells us that an object is simply a "named" instance of a specific class. For example, our E/R model contains a POLICY entity. (Note that the terms "class" and "entity" are synonymous.) There may be many different instances of the POLICY class, each one describing a successive refinement in the type of policy.

We may have automobile policies, life insurance policies, and so on; and each of these objects has different data items and, of course, different behaviors.

The behavior FILE_CLAIM will be dramatically different for a homeowner policy than for an auto policy, but from a database viewpoint, FILE_CLAIM serves one function. Several objects within a

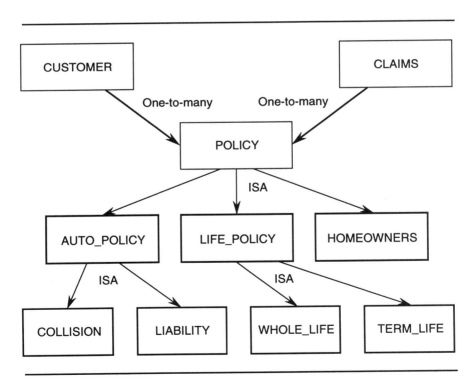

Figure 3.18.   Insurance policy.

class may also share behaviors. All of the policies will have a VERIFY_ELIGIBILITY behavior, but they would have drastically different procedures. Other behaviors are unique to an object (i.e., it would not make sense to associate a GET_DEATH_CERTIFICATE behavior with a LIABILITY object).

Essentially, an object-oriented database requires that different "types" or instances of each class be identified, and that the behaviors associated with these objects are identified. For example, the ITEM class within Guttbaum's hamburger stand has many attributes, some of which are shared and some which are unique. The "color" attribute within the ITEM class applies to the TOYS object within the BIG_MEAL object, but is not necessary for the food-related objects.

Due to the inherent complexity of object-oriented databases, a diagram is essential to the database designer. Consider the simplified database diagram in Figure 3.19. This diagram shows the class hierarchy, and relationships between the classes, and the instances (objects) within each class. For databases with limited domains, this type of diagram is very useful tool for visualizing the data relationships and objects.

The problem with this type of diagram is that there is nothing to describe the behaviors of the objects within the system. This is intentional. An entity/relation model, as originally defined by Dr. Chen in 1976, was only intended to depict the data tables and the relationships between the tables. While the data behaviors are indeed a component of the object-oriented database, they *are not* a data component of the model. The introduction of object-oriented databases only adds the new data requirement of objects within each class, and the ISA relationship does not do a good job at representing the third dimension that the E/R model must depict.

3.12.1. Construction Techniques for Object Behavior

In order to create a well-functioning object-oriented database, careful attention must be paid to the behaviors of the data within the model. Each behavior for each object must be carefully analyzed, and the hierarchy of behaviors must be determined.

In traditional object-oriented systems, the term "event" is

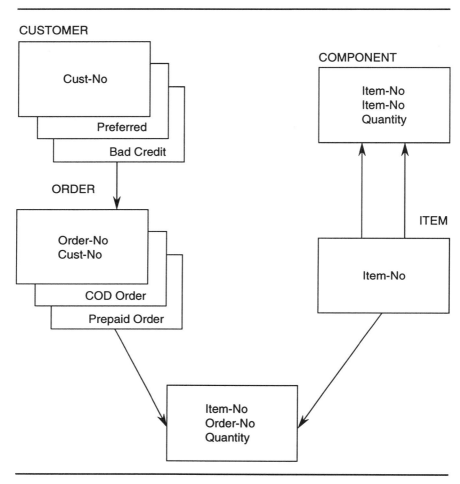

Figure 3.19. E/R diagram: Guttbaum's Hamburgers.

used to describe the behavior of an object. Events such as PLACE_AN_ORDER and COMPUTE_DISCOUNT take place within the predefined domain of the object-oriented system.

For database modeling it is far simpler to refer to events as they apply to the change to the database. From a database perspective, an event serves to either INSERT, UPDATE, or DELETE an object in the database. With this terminology, we can describe PLACE_AN_ORDER as an INSERT event behavior, and COMPUTE_DISCOUNT as an UPDATE event.

For example, the behavior PLACE_AN_ORDER, may operate on different data items and perform different procedures depending on the object. The object ĆOD_ORDER would "behave" in a different fashion than would object PREPAID_ORDER.

3.12.2. Inheritance

The issue of inheritance is also very important at this stage of object-oriented design. As one moves down the class hierarchy, data items and behaviors are inherited from their superclasses. The behavior PLACE_AN_ORDER may have a sub-behavior such as COMPUTE_DISCOUNT that depends on the data items of the CUSTOMER object to determine the discount. If the customer has a large volume of orders, it may have a greater discount than a new customer. The behavior PLACE_AN_ORDER inherits data items from the customer record such as CREDIT_RATING and SALES_STATUS.

From a database perspective, the behavior stores an object of the ORDER class, but the intermediate processing that determines the values within the order record is inherited from the CUSTOMER object. Under the object-oriented method, the lowest-level class is searched for the specified behavior, and if it is not found, its superclass is checked, and so on, until the requested behavior is located.

If we were using a traditional database, the process of checking credit and computing a sales discount might look like this:

```
IF CREDIT-RATING = 'POOR'
   MOVE 'COD' TO ORDER-TYPE
ELSE
 IF CREDIT-RATING = 'EXCELLENT'
   IF SALES-VOLUME > 10000
   COMPUTE DISCOUNT = ORDER-AMOUNT * .20
   ELSE COMPUTE DISCOUNT = ORDER-AMOUNT * .10
```

In plain English, if the customer has a poor credit rating, they receive no discount, and the order must be processed as a COD

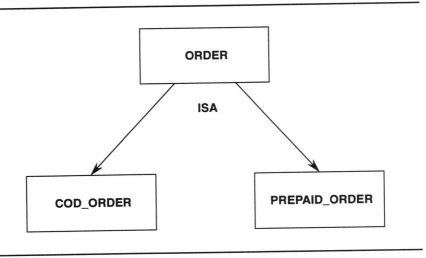

Figure 3.20.   Order class hierarchy.

order. If the customer does not have a poor credit rating, they will receive a 10% discount unless their order volume is greater then 10,000, in which case they receive a 20% discount.

This is a typical business rule that is usually coded into an application program. However, with an object-oriented approach, it is possible to incorporate the business rules and data items within the database engine, and simply PLACE_AN_ORDER. This "trigger" will start a subtask within the database that will perform the required computations and store the appropriate database records.

There are several ways to accomplish this. In a relational database, the data definitions of the customer and order records would include all necessary items, for all object classes, using the NULL value clause to compress out the unused items. This generic class definition is used with each object in the database, and the trigger is "fired" when the database directs the object to be stored. These triggers can be inserted into the schema definition for all data manipulation commands (DML), including INSERT, UPDATE, and DELETE.

3.13. POLYMORPHISM AND RELATIONAL DATABASES

Polymorphism is the ability of two different objects to behave differently when receiving the same message (behavior). The concept of polymorphism comes from the concept of "overloading," where a function may be used for several purposes. But how can this ability be incorporated in relational databases? In a relational database, behaviors are associated with data items with "triggers." Triggers invoke an operation before a specific database event happens to a record. If we have defined a relational table for each different class type in our generalization hierarchy, then we can associate "unique" behaviors with each of these tables.

PROBLEMS AND EXERCISES

1. Design a class hierarchy for each of the following entity classes:

    a. An "employee" class within your company
    b. A "vehicle" class at a car dealership
    c. An "item" class for a garden nursery shop

2. Given the following description, provide an E/R model and show all ISA relationships.

    ABC Computer Company serves the Nome, Alaska area with computer services. ABC has 50 employees, each of which has a variety of computer skills. When things get busy, ABC goes to a temporary agency for additional people. ABC works on many different kinds of projects, ranging from very small to huge (which require their entire programming team). The general manager likes to categorize the skill-sets of his people into managerial and technical categories. Employees with managerial skills are often called upon to manage small teams when a large project is undertaken and, after the completion of the project, they return to their technical skills. Because ABC deals with both hardware and software, each employee has been rated for proficiency in several areas of hardware technology, including LAN setup and PC configuration. Software technicians are rated for their programming skills, which may include relational database or object-oriented database.

3. Prepare a data flow diagram that would be appropriate for the following scenario. Be sure to identify all objects and behaviors associated with the objects.

The central billing department at the University of Peru uses the following procedure when a request for a computer item is received. All departments within the university are required to order their supplies from the billing department, and the department maintains a list of acceptable vendors. Incoming items are checked against the vendor lists. Those appearing on the list are checked off and approved for purchase. Those items not on the vendor lists are used in a bidding process. Offers for bids are sent out to the five vendors who have had the most business in the past year, and the lowest of the bids is accepted.

In many cases, a request will contain many items, some of which are on the approved list, and others that will require bids. In these cases, the request is back-ordered, and the available items are sent immediately. Occasionally, none of the five vendors will make a bid to sell an item, and the university will then allow the requesting department to purchase the item from any source.

REFERENCES

Abiteoul, S., Kanellkis, P., Waller, E., "Method schemas," *Communications of the ACM,* 1990.

Banerjee, J., "Data model issues for object-oriented applications," *ACM Transactions on Office Information Systems,* 5(1):3–26, 1987.

Bradley, J., "An object-relationship diagrammatic technique for object-oriented database definitions," *Journal of Database Administration,* Vol. 3, Issue 2, Spring 1992.

Brathwaite, K., *Object-Oriented Database Design: Concepts and Applications* (San Diego, CA: Academic Press, 1993).

Bratsberg, S.E., "FOOD: supporting explicit relations in a fully object-oriented database," Proceedings of the IFIP TC2/WG 2.6 Working Conference, 1991.

Cattel, R.G.G., Rogers, T., "Combining object-oriented and relational models of data," International Workshop on Object-Oriented Database Systems, Proceedings, Wash., DC, IEEE Computer Society Press, 1986.

Chung, Y., Fischer, G., "Illustration of object-oriented databases for the structure of a bill of materials," *Computers in Industry*, Vol. 19, June 1992.

Gane, C., Sarson, T., Structured Systems Analysis: Tools & Techniques, St. Louis, Improved Systems Technology.

Gorman, K., Choobineh, J., "An overview of the object-oriented entity relationship model (OOERM)," Proceedings of the Twenty-Third Annual Hawaii International Conference on Information Systems (Vol. 3), 336–345, 1991.

Goutas, S., Soupos, P., Christodoulakis, D., " Formalization of object-oriented database model with rules," *Information and Software Technology*, Vol. 33, Dec. 1991.

Martin, J., Odell, J., *Object-Oriented Analysis and Design* (Englewood Cliffs, NJ: Prentice-Hall Publishers, 1992).

McFadden, F., "Conceptual design of object-oriented databases," *Journal of Object-Oriented Programming*, Vol. 4, Sept. 1991.

Ruben, K., Goldberg, A., "Object behavior analysis," *Communications of the ACM*, Sept. 1992.

Thalheim, B., "Extending the entity-relationship model for a high-level, theory-based database design," International Workshop on Object-Oriented Database Systems, Proceedings, Wash., DC, IEEE Computer Society Press, 1990.

4

Complex Many-to-Many and Recursive Class Hierarchies

4.1   MANY-TO-MANY RELATIONSHIPS

There are many real-world situations where many-to-many data relationships exist between data entities. Some of these many-to-many relationships are "recursive," that is, a class may have a many-to-many relationship with other objects within the same class.

In order to properly model an object-oriented database, a method must be introduced to identify and incorporate these types of data relationships into the overall model.

Examples of many-to-many relationships include:

STUDENT-CLASS—a student may take many classes, and a class contains many students.

ORDER-ITEM—an order may contain many items, and an item may participate in many orders.

These many-to-many relationships require a "junction" class type. Note that this junction record must contain the primary key values of the "owner" tables.

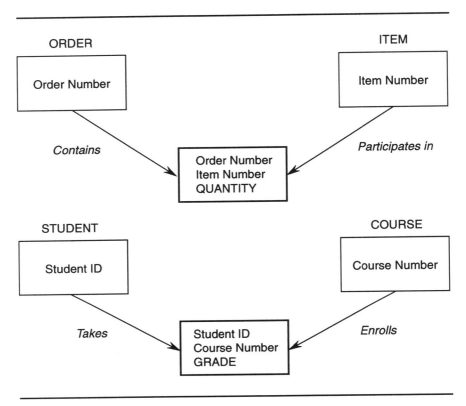

Figure 4.1. Many-to-many relationships.

4.2. MULTIPLE INHERITANCE AND JUNCTION RECORDS

Whenever a many-to-many relationship exists, the problem of multiple inheritance must be addressed. For example, whenever an object of the GRADE record has an event (INSERT, UPDATE), it will inherit data and behaviors from the STUDENT class as well as the COURSE class. In the example of the order database, as each item is added for an order, a LINE_ITEM object is stored, and it will inherit the data and behaviors from the ORDER and the ITEM classes.

When a student registers for a course, a set of rules, or behav-

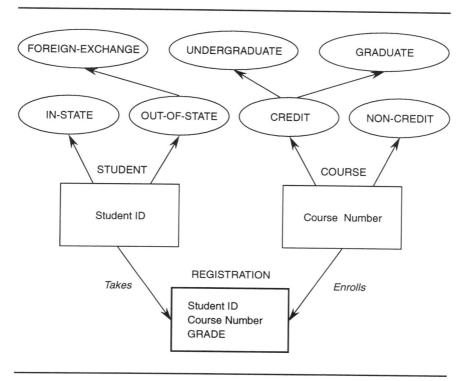

Figure 4.2.   Class hierarchy with E/R model.

iors, are invoked. In this example, two sets of behaviors are required for a student registration. A review of the rules makes it
clear that inherited data items will affect the way that a student
registration is handled within this database:

Registration method:

—Only graduate students may enroll in graduate-level courses.
—Undergraduates must have successfully completed at least
60 hours in order to qualify to take an upper-division course.

Tuition computation method:

—Graduate-level courses cost $500 for an in-state student,
and $1000 for out-of-state.

—Undergraduate courses cost $400 for an in-state student, and $800 for out-of-state.

—Foreign exchange students pay the out-of-state rate less 30%.

As you can see, the data items that are inherited from other classes are going to affect the registration and tuition computation.

It is important to conceptualize the differences between the manipulation of objects and the manipulation of rows and columns in a relational database.

We see that the "report card" is a collection of rows from the STUDENT, REGISTRATION, and COURSE tables. Within the object-oriented database, a report card is treated as a finite identity, and the components of the report card will never be referenced except through the behaviors that are associated with a report card.

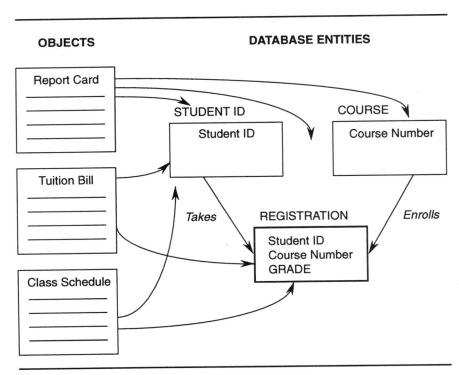

Figure 4.3   Objects are composed of many database entities.

4.3. RECURSIVE MANY-TO-MANY DATA RELATIONSHIPS

Recursive many-to-many data relationships also provide inheritance. Consider the example of CLASS-PREREQUISITE. Assume that we have the following hierarchy of classes and prerequisites.

This figure describes a course-prerequisite hierarchy for a university. Note that the is-a-prerequisite-for relationships are relatively straightforward, indicating which courses are required to

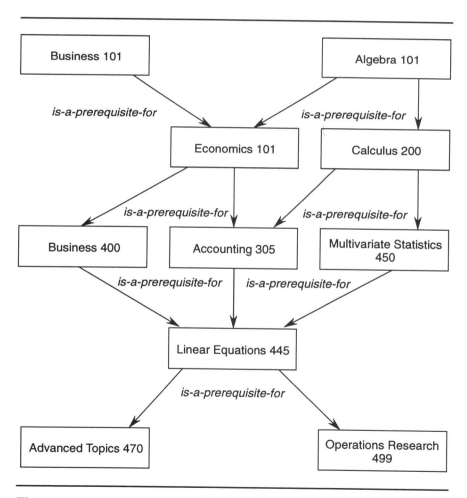

Figure 4.4. Recursive courses with prerequisites.

take a course. For example, the prerequisites for Linear Equations 445 are Business 400, Accounting 305, and Multivariate Statistics 450. These courses also have prerequisites, which may in turn have prerequisites, and so on, ad infinitum. We could "explode" the prerequisites for Linear Equations 445 as follows.

Bill-of-materials explosion for: Linear Equations 445			
Prerequisite	*Prerequisite*	*Prerequisite*	*Topic*
Business 400			Financial management
	Econ 101		Macro-economics
		Business 101	General management
		Algebra 101	Quadratic equations
Accounting 305			FASB regulations
	Econ 101		Macro-economics
		Business 101	General management
		Algebra 101	Quadratic equations
	Calculus 200		Integral calculus
		Algebra 101	Quadratic equations
Multivariate Statistics 450			SPSS modeling
	Calculus 200		Integral calculus
		Algebra 101	Quadratic equations

If we were going to develop an object-oriented system to keep track of the prerequisite courses, we would need to develop a data structure that would provide for multiple inheritance. Multiple inheritance would be required as we traversed the levels of the recursive relationship.

Each occurrence of a COURSE object will have different topics, and an object-oriented implementation must be able to iterate through all courses until it reaches "terminus," where the course has no further prerequisites.

Unfortunately, the recursive many-to-many relationship is very confusing and almost impossible to understand without the aid of a graphical representation. Students have suggested that these are called bill-of-material "explosions" because this is what happens to their brain cells when you try to comprehend these relationships.

A nineteenth-century Professor, Augustus DeMorgan, described the recursive many-to-many relationship with a very entertaining poem:

Great fleas have little fleas upon their backs to bite 'em,
And little fleas have lesser fleas, and so, ad infinitum.

The great fleas themselves, in turn, have greater fleas to go on,
While these, in turn, have greater still, and greater still, and so on.

4.4   GRAPHICAL TOOLS

Recursive data relationships are very common, and any object-oriented database must be able to represent this data structure. Other examples of the recursive many-to-many relationship would include:

Part (component)	A part has many components. A part may be a component in many parts.
Coourt Case (cite)	A judge's opinion cites related cases. That case may later be cited in subsequent court cases

The relationship:

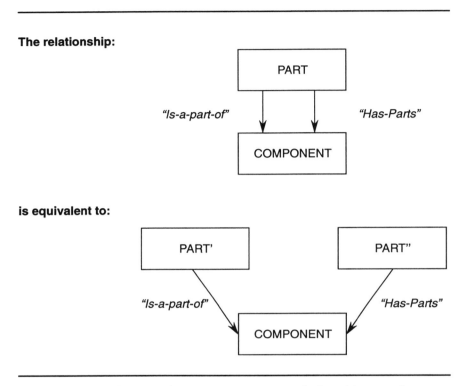

is equivalent to:

Figure 4.5.   A recursive many-to-many relationship may be
graphed as a many-to-many relationship.

It is helpful to visualize the recursive many-to-many relationship as an ordinary many-to-many relationship with the owner
entity "pulled apart" into owner1 and owner2. This figure shows
how the junction entity is used to establish the relationship.

There is no substitute for a graphical picture to help to conceptualize a recursive many-to-many relationship. In the
CODASYL model, these are called "set occurrence" diagrams,
and they show the pointer chains that are used to link the relationships. For relational databases, table sketches are used to
show the junction table that contains both an implosion and an

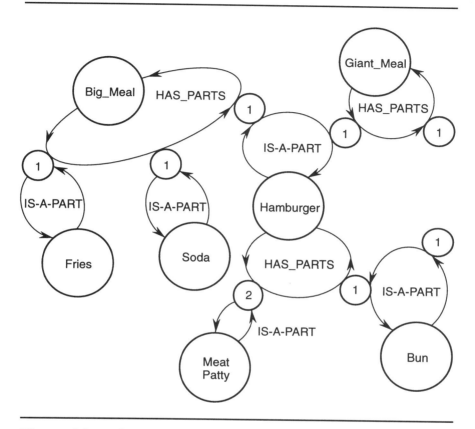

Figure 4.6.   Set occurrence diagram: recursive many-to-many relationship.

explosion column. Students find that the set occurrence diagram is very helpful for understanding data relationships.

In the above figure, it is easy to see how the database would be navigated to determine the components for a Big_Meal. To navigate this diagram, start at the object Big_Meal and follow the HAS_PARTS link to the bubble containing the number 1. This is the quantity for the item, and following this bubble's IS-A-PART link tells us that 1 Fries are included in a Big_Meal. Now we return to the HAS_PARTS link for Big_Meal and find the next bubble, whose IS-A-PART link tells us that one soda participates in a Big_Meal. We continue this process until we do not find any more entities in the HAS_PARTS relationship. In sum, the HAS_PARTS relationships indicate that a Big_Meal consists of one order of fries, one soda, and one hamburger. We also see that the hamburger consists of two meat patties and one bun.

You can also see how the database can be navigated to determine which parts use a specific component. For example, we can start at the hamburger bubble, and navigate the IS-A-PART relationships to see that one hamburger participates in the Giant_Meal and one in the Big_Meal.

Recursive relationships are also indicated. For example, if we were listing the components of a Big Meal, all components would also be displayed.

Bill-of-material explosion for: Big Meal			
PART1	*PART2*	*PART3*	*Quantity*
Hamburger			1
	Meat Patty		2
		Pork	4 oz.
		Beef	3 oz.
	Bun		1
Fries			1 order
	Potato		1
	Grease		1 cup
Soda			1
	Ice		1/2 cup
	Drink		1/3 cup

Conversely, the recursion association could be applied to any item to see which items it participates in. For example, grease is used in:

Bill-of-material implosion for: Grease

PART1	PART2	PART3
Fries		
		Big Meal
		Giant Meal
Meat Patty		
	Hamburger	
		Big Meal
		Giant Meal
	Cheeseburger	
	Big Zac	
Fried Pies		
		Giant Meal

Even though these are quite simple examples, there are many object-oriented systems that have items with many subassemblies, and these recursions may go dozens of levels down in the hierarchy.

Consider an object-oriented database to manage fast food items. All nonfood items will have a class to hold all of their data and behaviors. This is an example of an "abstract" class, because no object of NON_FOOD_PART would even be created. NON_FOOD_PART does include ordering behaviors and the names of suppliers, but these will be inherited by the lower-level classes, namely the TOY_PART and PAPER_PART objects. Next in the class hierarchy we would find the TOY_PART class, which also has data and behaviors, and unlike the NON_FOOD_PART "abstract" class, TOY_PART is a "concrete" class. As we know, a concrete class will have objects, and all objects of TOY_PART class will inherit the data and behaviors from the NON_FOOD_PART class.

Many designers do not fully understand the difference between these recursive relationships and the concept of inherit-

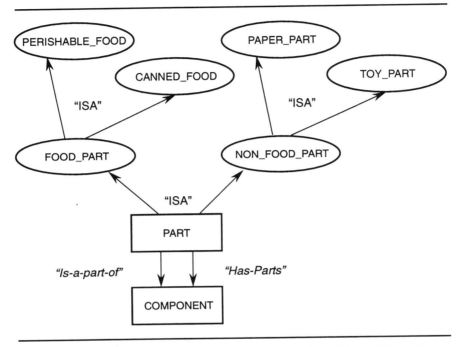

Figure 4.7.   Recursive many-to-many relationships with ISA hierarchy.

ance. With inheritance, an object inherits data and behaviors from one or more superclasses. With recursive relationships, an object may inherit from dozens of other objects in the hierarchy. For example, assume we have the relationship in Figure 4.8.

This hierarchical representation of the recursive objects shows the "has-parts" relationship as we move down from large parts to smaller parts. While this is very useful for conceptualizing the explosion side of recursion, we do not see the "implosion" of the recursion. The ability to see this "where-used" side may be very useful for planning. For example, if we need to plan the quantity to order for a small part, say, grease, we could walk the implosive side of the relationship to determine which parts use grease, and determine the quantity of grease used by the sum of these parts.

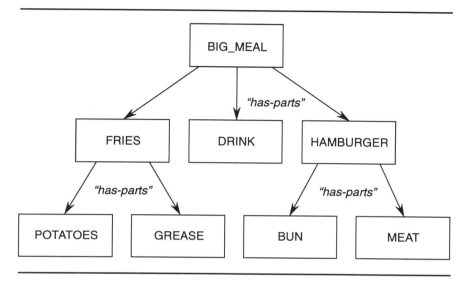

Figure 4.8. Recursion may be represented as a hierarchy.

4.5. SUMMARY

These complex data relationships are often overlooked in the design of object-oriented systems, and many database designers, failing to see a simple solution, either ignore the complex relationships or create duplicitous data structures to manage implosion and explosion. By recognizing the internal constructs behind many-to-many and recursive many-to-many data relationships, we can confidently model and implement object-oriented databases that accurately reflect real-world data relationships.

PROBLEMS AND EXERCISES

1. Using the customer-order diagram shown in Figure 4.9, answer the following questions:

   A. All of the pens we have sold in the past year are defective and we must send out recall letters to all customers who have ordered pens. Prepare a set of procedural navigation statements that would identify the quantity and orders for which pens participate.

B. Management has requested a summary of all of our orders for the past year. This report will sweep all customers, find all of their orders, and for each order, scan each item, determining the price and computing the total. Total amounts will be calculated for each order, for each customer, and for all customers. Prepare a set of navigation statements that would show how you would navigate the data to arrive at an answer.

2. The most complex data structure is the recursive many-to-many relationship where the owner entity has an embedded

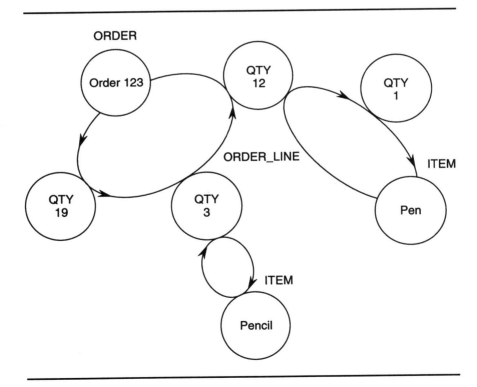

Figure 4.9. Customer database.

ISA class hierarchy. Draw a pictorial representation for the following scenario, making sure that you have identified all of the ISA relationships between the entities.

Mancato State University is considering an object-oriented system to assist with their registration system. The registration system uses the entities of STUDENT, COURSE, GRADE, and PREREQ as the base entities, but no object-oriented constructs have been added to the structure. The registration process involves several processes. When a student asks to be enrolled into a course, the student's prior course history is checked for the necessary prerequisites. If he or she is qualified to enter the class, the system then checks to see if the course is CREDIT or NON_CREDIT. CREDIT courses are divided into CORE and NON_CORE courses, and some CORE courses must be taken together with another course, even though both courses may have the same prerequisites. In addition to meeting these criteria, a student must be enrolled in the proper college in order to enroll for upper-division courses. For example, only members of the Business or Engineering College are allowed to enroll in upper-division business courses.

3. Consider the recursive relationship between an employee and the employees that they supervise. An employee may supervise many employees, and at the same time be supervised by another employee, namely, his or her boss. Use the organizational chart for the company where you work (or a company that you are familiar with) to represent the recursion as:

1. An explosion
2. An implosion
3. A set occurrence diagram

REFERENCES

Banerjee, J., "Data model issues for object-oriented applications," *ACM Transactions on Office Information Systems*, 5(1):3–26, 1987.

Bradley, J., "An object-relationship diagrammatic technique for object-oriented database definitions," *Journal of Database Administration*, Vol. 3, Issue 2, Spring 1992.

Brathwaite, K., *Object-Oriented Database Design: Concepts and Applications* (San Diego, CA: Academic Press, 1993).

Burleson, D., Kassicieh, S., Lievano, R. "Design and implementation of a decision support system for academic scheduling," *Information and Management*, Volume II, Number 2, Sept. 1986.

McFadden, F., "Conceptual design of object-oriented databases," *Journal of Object-Oriented Programming*, Vol. 4, Sept. 1991.

Thalheim, B., "Extending the entity-relationship model for a high-level, theory-based database design," International Workshop on Object-Oriented Database Systems, Proceedings, Wash., DC, IEEE Computer Society Press, 1990.

5

Designing Dynamic Class Hierarchies

Most commercial databases are adequate for static object-oriented databases, where each class can be defined in advance. But what about the circumstances where database is dynamic and requires new classes? Such a database must have a facility for modifying the existing class hierarchy and adding new classes into an existing hierarchy. Under this scenario, the database must be directed to "store" classes with a new set of data attributes, and to dynamically associate behaviors with these new classes.

5.1. INTRODUCTION

This "self-defining" capability is best suited to very dynamic databases in which the data attributes and behaviors change frequently. CAD/CAM systems are a good example of an application where new objects are created and incorporated into other objects in a class hierarchy.

Some vendors have recognized the need to create new classes. The IBM OS/2 version 2 operating system now offers a "system object model" (SOM), which claims to offer an environment for the development of object-oriented class libraries. Novel classes can be added to the model at any time, and existing behaviors and data items can be combined to form new object classes. The

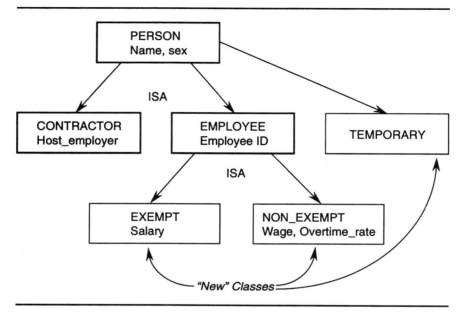

Figure 5.1.   Dynamic addition of new classes to the hierarchy.

objects from these new classes may be shared by other OS/2 applications and exported to external systems. Microsoft is also promising a similar feature with "Cairo," the next generation of the Windows NT operating system.

Many commercial databases offer "repositories," "catalogs," or "data dictionaries," which serve to store the metadata for the system. This information might include the data types and the sizes of all data items within a table, referential integrity rules, and so on. To create a self-defining class structure, new system tables will need to be created to hold the new entities. Just as many relational databases have a SYSTABLES table, which contains table definition information, we need to define a SYSCLASS table to hold information about our classes. A SYSCLASS table may have many subclasses that are also of type SYSCLASS, and an instance of SYSCLASS may participate as a member of a larger class. This is a recursive many-to-many relationship. This model can also support multiple inheritance because a SYSCLASS may be a member of more than one superclass.

Figure 5.2 shows a many-to-many relationship between a SYSCLASS and SYSBEHAVIOR. A class may be associated with many behaviors, and a behavior may participate in many classes. We also require a recursive relationship within the BEHAVIOR record. This is necessary to represent the situation where behaviors are "nested" (i.e., PLACE_ORDER consists of CHECK_CREDIT and CHECK_INVENTORY). A behavior may contain many behaviors, and at the same time participate as a sub-behavior within a larger assembly of behaviors. For example, CHECK-CREDIT may participate within several behaviors, such as PLACE_ORDER and MODIFY_ORDER.

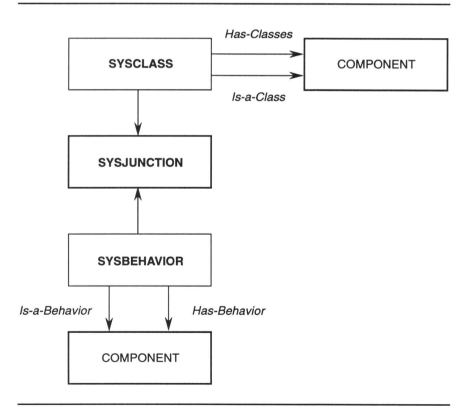

Figure 5.2.   Entity/relationship model for object-oriented systems.

To use the object-oriented paradigm with relational tables, all of these table structures will need to be defined. Once defined, these tables will be used to govern the use of classes and objects within the object-oriented database.

Bear in mind that creating and integrating these tables into the design can be very time-consuming and expensive. In many cases, this cost does not justify the benefits, especially for static databases. Most business systems are relatively static and do not require frequent additions of object classes, and when changes are required, the Database Administrator can quickly change the class hierarchy definitions.

In order to be truly self-defining, the database must allow for the creation of new classes, associating the new class with super-classes and defining the attributes and behaviors of the new class. Because the new object is always associated with an existing class, all relationships to other classes are predefined, and the new object will automatically inherit any behaviors associated with its superclasses.

The creation of "self-defining" classes is a relatively simple task within most commercial database systems. Self-defining classes, in the context of this discussion, relates to the ability of the database to dynamically generate CREATE TABLE statements, and to the ability to associate behaviors and events with each table. For example, a university database may have a STUDENT class, with associated subclasses for in-state students and out-of-state students. A self-defining database would allow for the insertion of a new STUDENT subclass, such as foreign exchange students. The class FOREIGN_EXCHANGE_STUDENT would be defined to the database together with its shared and unique data items, and all associated superclasses.

For a relational database to support the dynamic creation of objects, there must be three system tables to manage the object schema. These tables are called SYSCLASS, SYSOBJECTS, and SYSBEHAVIORS. The SYSCLASS table contains the class name, the primary key, and the key picture for all classes defined to the database. SYSOBJECTS contains the object name and the associated class name. The SYSBEHAVIORS table contains the class name, the object name, and a row for each behavior associated with the object, usually INSERT, DELETE, and UPDATE.

SYSTABLE Table

TABLE_NAME	PRIMARY_KEY	CARDINALITY
CUSTOMER	CUST_NO	NUMBER
ORDER	ORDER_NO	NUMBER
ITEM	ITEM_NO	NUMBER

SYSCLASS Table

TABLE_NAME	CLASS_NAME
CUSTOMER	PREFERRED_CUSTOMER
CUSTOMER	REGULAR_CUSTOMER
ORDER	COD_ORDER
ORDER	PREPAID_ORDER

SYSJUNCTION Table

CLASS_NAME	BEHAVIOR_NAME
COD_ORDER	CHECK_INVENTORY
REGULAR_CUSTOMER	PLACE_ORDER

SYSBEHAVIOR Table

BEHAVIOR_NAME	TYPE	BEHAVIOR
CHECK_INVENTORY	SELECT	Move...
PLACE_ORDER	UPDATE	Move...
ADD_CUSTOMER	INSERT	Move...
CHECK_CREDIT	SELECT	Move...

These tables can manage all environmental factors related to any object within the database schema. But how do we create an interface which allows these tables to be populated, and how do we ensure that these tables are used by the system?

Following is a sample screen that shows how new classes may be defined.

```
Class Name: _____
within class: _____
            _____
            _____

Data Item Name              Picture
_____        _____
_____        _____
_____        _____

"Insert" Behavior: _____
"Delete" Behavior: _____
"Update" Behavior: _____
```

To understand the underlying data structures behind this approach, let's look at the behavior of the relational tables when a new object is added to an existing class.

The following processes must occur as the new object is added:

1. Verify that the specified superclasses exist.
2. Get the primary key for the class record.
3. Execute the CREATE TABLE syntax.
4. Add the new object to the SYSOBJECTS table.
5. Insert the new behaviors into the BEHAVIOR TABLE.

Assume that we are adding a new type of customer: a "preferred" customer who will receive special discounts on orders. We will create a new class called PREFERRED within the CUSTOMER class, and add the appropriate attributes and behaviors to this class. Assume that a preferred customer will receive overnight delivery of all orders, and also receive an additional 5% discount

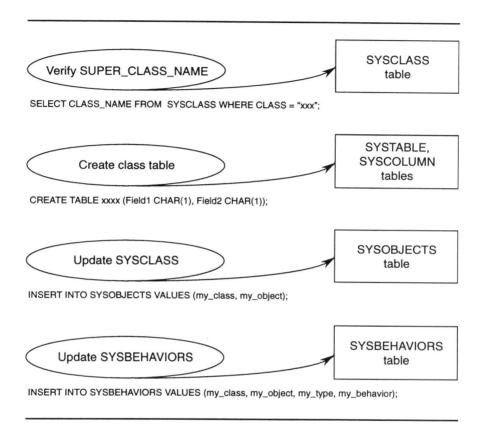

Figure 5.3. Procedure for adding a new class.

of the total order amount. In addition, the order amounts of preferred customers are tracked and special gifts are awarded to all
preferred customers who order more than $5000 per year. The
preferred customer may choose between a watch or a briefcase.
Following is what the screen to add this object might look like:

Class Name: ___PREFERRED_____
within class: ___CUSTOMER_____

```
Data Item Name            Picture
YTD_PURCHASES             NUMBER
GIFT_PREFERENCE           CHAR(30)
```

"Insert" Behavior: MOVE OS_FIELD TO
                   GIFT_PREFERENCE
"Delete" Behavior:
"Update" Behavior: ADD ORDER AMOUNT TO YTD
                   PURCHASES

Step 1—Check for valid superclass and get superclass primary key:

```
    SELECT PRIMARY_KEY, PICTURE INTO my_key, my_pic from
SYSCLASS WHERE CLASS = super_class;

    IF NOT_FOUND() THEN
         @ 1,1 say 'Invalid class. Please re-enter'
    ENDIF
```

Execute CREATE TABLE Syntax:

```
SQL="CREATE TABLE " + my_object + " ( " +
    my_key + " " + my_pic +
    " PRIMARY KEY NOT NULL REFERENCES " +
    my_class + "." + my_key + " , "
    my_field1 + " " + picture1 + " , " +
    my_field2 + " " + picture2 + " ); "
&SQL
```

This will generate the SYNTAX:

```
CREATE TABLE PREFERRED_CUSTOMER
(CUST_NO        NUMBER PRIMARY KEY NOT NULL
               REFERENCES CUSTOMER.CUST_NO,
```

```
YTD_PURCHASES      NUMBER,
GIFT_PREFERENCE    CHAR(20));
```

Step 2—Add new object to SYSCLASS table:

```
SQL = "INSERT INTO SYSCLASS VALUES (my_class, my_class)"
```

This will generate the SYNTAX:

```
INSERT INTO SYSCLASS VALUES (my_class, my_class);
```

Step 3—Add behaviors to SYSBEHAVIOR table:

```
SQL="INSERT INTO SYSBEHAVIOR VALUES (" +
    my_class, + my_object + my_type + my_behavior + ");"
```

This will generate the SYNTAX:

```
    INSERT     INTO      SYSBEHAVIOR       VALUES
(CUSTOMER,
PREFERRED_CUSTOMER, INSERT, 'MOVE OS_FIELD TO ...');
```

We now have a framework for the new PREFERRED_CUSTOMER class, and objects within this class will be referenced by the database in the same fashion as any other object within the CUSTOMER class. For example, let's examine the online screen that adds a new customer:

Customer Name: _____
Customer Address: _____

_____
_____

Customer Type: (choose one)
    ( ) PREFERRED_CUSTOMER
    ( ) REGULAR_CUSTOMER
    ( ) PROSPECTIVE_CUSTOMER

The valid choices for the customer type are gathered from the SYSOBJECT table and are mapped into this screen. Our new customer object will appear on this screen immediately after it has been defined as a subclass within the customer class.

The relational syntax behind the scenes will select the SYSCLASS table:

```
SELECT TABLE_NAME FROM SYSCLASS
    WHERE CLASS = CUSTOMER;
```

When a new customer is added, the code will interrogate the customer type selection and perform whatever behaviors are assigned to this object in the SYSBEHAVIOR table.

```
SELECT BEHAVIOR into SQL from SYSBEHAVIOR
    WHERE TYPE = 'INSERT' and OBJECT_NAME = my_choice;
&SQL
```

In many relational systems such as dBASE and FoxPro, the ampersand (&) operator can be used to execute the contents of a variable. In the above case, the SQL extracts a database command from a table, and the &SQL command is used to execute this command.

Note that we have removed all DML processing from the application code. Any database-related work is stored in SYSBEHAVIOR, and the application module becomes nothing more than a driver to this table. The benefits of this approach are now very clear. When modifications to the existing system are necessary, just change the row in SYSBEHAVIOR, and the application driver never requires modification.

5.2. INHERITANCE

When an object is accessed at runtime, it must access, or inherit, all of the behaviors and data attributes of its superclasses. Let's take a look at how this happens. In our university example, the REGISTRATION behavior serves to CHECK_STATUS, ENROLL_STUDENT, and COMPUTE_TUITION.

These three sub-behaviors are nested beneath the REGISTRATION behavior via the COMPONENT table as follows.

SYSBEHAVIOR Table

BEHAVIOR_NAME	TYPE	BEHAVIOR
REGISTER_STUDENT		
CHECK_STATUS	SELECT	Move...
ENROLL_STUDENT	INSERT	Move...
COMPUTE_TUITION	UPDATE	Move...

Component Table

IS_A_BEHAVIOR	HAS_BEHAVIOR
REGISTER_STUDENT	CHECK_STATUS
REGISTER_STUDENT	ENROLL_STUDENT
REGISTER_STUDENT	COMPUTE_TUITION
ENROLL_STUDENT	FIND_TYPE
ENROLL_STUDENT	LOOKUP_TRANSCRIPT

This relationship could also be viewed as a set occurrence diagram as shown in Figure 5.4.

As you see, some behaviors within our relational tables are nested several levels deep. In order to invoke the REGISTRATION behavior we will make the following calls to the database:

```
REGISTER =
    (
    COMPUTE_TUITION
    + ENROLL_STUDENT
    + CHECK_STATUS =
        (
        FIND_TYPE
        + LOOKUP_TRANSCRIPT
        )
    )
```

The above syntax clearly shows how the behaviors are nested, but how do we make our relational tables behave in this fashion?

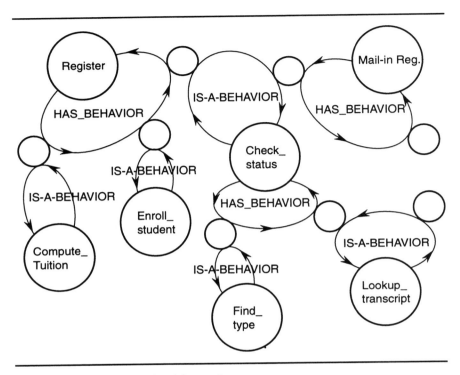

Figure 5.4. Behavior hierarchy.

The ultimate result of this behavior is the insertion of a row into the Registration table, so a trigger (or a DBRM) could be added to the insert on registration. The following chapter contains a complete discussion of triggers and DBRMs.

```
Create trigger REGISTRATION
      BEFORE INSERT OF REGISTRATION
for each row
  SELECT BEHAVIOR INTO :behavior
  FROM SYSBEHAVIOR A, COMPONENT B, COMPONENT C
  WHERE BEHAVIOR_NAME = 'REGISTRATION' and
          A.BEHAVIOR_NAME = B.IS_A_BEHAVIOR and
          B.IS_A_BEHAVIOR = C.IS_A_BEHAVIOR;

      /* now, execute the variable :behavior */
      &behavior
```

This trigger should recursively descend to all of the levels in the nesting structure, executing each behavior variable as it is encountered. Of course, this requires an interpretative relational database such as FoxPro®, because the contents of the behavior field is executed as a database command.

5.3.   SUMMARY

While not an object-oriented database in its purest form, these techniques can be applied to any relational database. By storing the behaviors in relational tables, the application programs become nothing more than single SQL statements that "fire" a predefined trigger or DBRM. This method is very useful for systems that change frequently.

REFERENCES

Cattell, R.G.G., *Object Data Management: Object-Oriented and Extended Relational Database Systems* (Reading, MA: Addison-Wesley, 1991).

Cattel, R.G.G., Rogers, T., "Combining object-oriented and relational models of data," International Workshop on Object-Oriented Database Systems, Proceedings, Wash., DC, IEEE Computer Society Press, 1986.

Codd, E.F., *The Relational Model for Database Management* Version 2 (Reading, MA: Addison-Wesley, 1990).

Loomis, M., "Integrating objects with relational technology," *Object Magazine*, July/August 1991.

Loomis, M., "Object and Relational technology. Can they cooperate?," *Object Magazine*, July/August 1991.

Vasan, R., "Relational databases and objects: a hybrid solution," *Object Magazine*, July/August 1991.

Yourdon, E., "The marriage of relational and object-oriented design," *Relational Journal*, Vol. 3, Issue 6, Jan. 1992.

Simulating Object-Oriented Databases with Triggers

6.1. TRIGGERS

Many database systems now support the use of "triggers" that can be fired at specific events. The insert, modification, or deletion of a record may fire a trigger; or business events, such as PLACE_ORDER, may initiate a trigger action. Oracle® Corporation claims that the design of their triggers closely follows the ANSI/ISO SQL3 draft standard (ANSI X3H6), but Oracle triggers are more robust in functionality than the ANSI standard. Triggers are defined at the schema level of the system, and will "fire" whenever an SQL select, update, delete, or insert command is issued.

Oracle triggers have the ability to call procedures, and a trigger may include SQL statements, thus providing the ability to "nest" SQL statements. Oracle triggers are stored as procedures that may be parameterized and used to simulate object-oriented behavior. For example, assume that we want to perform a behavior called CHECK_TOTAL_INVENTORY whenever an item is added to an order.

The trigger definition would be:

```
Create trigger CHECK_TOTAL_INVENTORY
        AFTER SELECT OF ITEM
```

141

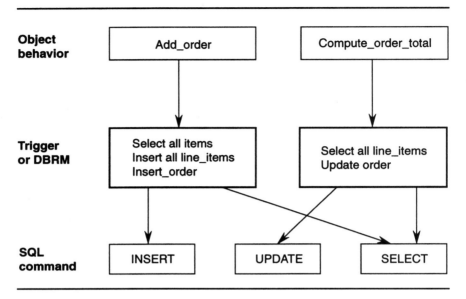

Figure 6.1. Objects, triggers, and SQL.

```
for each row

   SELECT COUNT(*) INTO :count
   FROM QUANTITY WHERE ITEM_# = :myitem:

IF :count < ITEM.TOTAL then
   ......
END IF;
```

Triggers could also be combined to handle combined events, such as the reordering of an ITEM when the quantity-on-hand falls below a predefined level:

```
CREATE TRIGGER reorder BEFORE UPDATE on ITEM
 FOR EACH ROW WHEN (new.reorderable = 'Y')
    BEGIN
        IF new.qty_on_hand + old.qty_on_order <
           new.minimum_qty
        THEN
```

```
                        INSERT INTO REORDER VALUES (item_nbr,
                           reorder_qty);
                        new.qty_on_order := old.qty_on_order +
                           reorder_qty;
             END IF;
       END
```

Ingres corporation now offers an Object Management option for their popular Ingres database. Object Management, as defined by Ingres, allows for the creation of user-defined data types. Once defined, these types and functions may be used in standard SQL statements.

6.2. DATABASE REQUEST MODULES

Many databases allows for the insertion of *database request modules* (DBRMs), which can be included in the schema definition. These perform similarly to triggers and invoke a precompiled module whenever the DBRM is fired. Like triggers, DBRMs are attached at the database definition level and are associated with specific DML events. The DBRM may receive and pass parameters and data, which make them very flexible tools for the creation of object-oriented systems. For example, an IDMS schema definition may have a record called ORDER with the following definition:

```
ADD RECORD NAME IS ORDER
RECORD ID IS 1000
SHARE STRUCTURE OF ORDER-RECORD VERSION 1
LOCATION MODE IS CALC USING ORDER-NBR
WITHIN AREA ORDER-AREA OFFSET 0 PERCENT FOR 100
   PERCENT
CALL PLACEORD   BEFORE STORE
CALL MODORD     BEFORE MODIFY
CALL DELORDER   BEFORE ERASE.
```

In this example, the module PLACEORD would be called before any occurrence of an ORDER record would be stored in the database. PLACEORD could be used to check inventory levels for each item in the order or could be used to verify the credit of the customer who was placing the order. DBRMs are usually written in third-generation languages such as COBOL or FORTRAN, but some databases support the C language and Assembler.

The problem with DBRMs is the relationship between storing a record in a database and associating the DBRM to an object. An object may consist of many database records in different areas of the database, and care must be taken to ensure that the DBRM addresses all of the records that compose the object.

In this example, an ORDER object would consist of one OR-DER record and a series of LINE-ITEM records, one for each item on the order. The DBRM, PLACEORD could manage storing the ORDER record and then read each item, verifying inventory and adding the LINE-ITEM records.

6.3.   ENFORCING ENCAPSULATION

Using DBRMs and triggers is an extremely useful concept, but what do we do about the problem of encapsulation? As we know, the object-oriented paradigm requires that all data be accessed through its methods. We also know that a relational database has SQL, which permits ad hoc queries.

Most database designers would not be too worried about the possibility of an ad hoc update, but there is always a possibility that an object could be logically corrupted. For example, a data item that is encapsulated within a procedure could be easily altered to issue a global SQL update operation. If we are determined to enforce encapsulation for our relational database, we must "turn off" all SQL that has not already been handled through our triggers.

As you might guess, this is not a difficult chore. All we have to do is ensure that a trigger exists for EVERY possible SQL operation against EVERY table, and add a return-null condition to all undesired SQL operators.

With DBRMs we have a more serious problem. DBRMs are inserted in the schema of a CODASYL database to activate before or after a database event. For example, how could we nullify an insert operation on an entity when we can only specify operations that may occur before or after the insert? As it turns out, all operations from the time that the DBRM is called to the end of the transaction may be aborted with the ROLLBACK DML verb. All we have to do is to compile an online COBOL program with the single statement ROLLBACK. This technique can be used to disable all unwanted DML within our database.

```
ADD RECORD NAME IS ORDER
RECORD ID IS 1000
SHARE STRUCTURE OF ORDER-RECORD VERSION 1
LOCATION MODE IS CALC USING ORDER-NBR
WITHIN AREA ORDER-AREA OFFSET 0 PERCENT FOR 100 PERCENT
CALL ROLLBACK      AFTER STORE
CALL ROLLBACK      AFTER MODIFY
CALL ROLLBACK      AFTER ERASE.
```

6.4. SUMMARY

Triggers and DBRMs are extremely valuable database tools, even if we do not choose to use them for object-oriented implementation. All commercial databases offer some type of trigger whether they are called "user-exits" or DBRMs. It is always a good idea to consult the user manual for your database system to see what types of triggers you may use, and how they function.

Relational Databases and Object-Oriented Databases

7.1. INTRODUCTION

Many users of object-oriented languages are resorting to many different methods to achieve object persistence. The techniques range from self-made databases that store linked-list structures, to "front-ends" that are used to put the objects into a standard relational database.

Industry experts agree, as typified by Christopher Stone, President of the Object Management Group:

> So what the object database community needs—excuse me, what the object community needs—is agreement on a data model and how you pinpoint it for design, how do you build applications that are free from specific Data Manipulation Languages (DMLs). Does that mean that you extend SQL— and that's going on all over the place—to be object-oriented? Does it mean you develop an entirely new object query language? Probably not. Does it mean you just extend C++ and pray the marriage of a programming language and a database is really going to happen? I don't think that is going to happen. The writing is on the wall that it'll pretty much be an evolution of SQL. Object database technology,

those extensions to SQL supporting abstract data types, and things like that will become much more prevalent over the next two to three years. (Stone, 1992)

It should be very clear that some of the internal data structures of a C++ program could easily be replicated with a set of relational tables. Many C++ programmers use this approach to store their objects, and some have been very successful with this approach. Unfortunately, a static set of relational tables cannot handle the addition of new classes or objects without new tables being defined to support the new data structures.

Most C++ systems that interact with relational databases use a crude but effective compromise. They invoke a routine that populates all of the internal object structures when the system is started, and then regurgitates the object information back into the database at the conclusion of the session. More sophisticated approaches allow the C++ system to create new classes and objects, and send the appropriate CREATE TABLE statements to the database for processing.

Regardless of the approach, there is interest in using object-oriented programming with existing commercial databases. This chapter investigates some methods that can assist the object-oriented programmer in utilizing relational database systems.

7.2. CONCEPTUAL FRAMEWORK FOR OBJECT-ORIENTED/RELATIONAL DATABASES

When attempting to reconcile the object-oriented approach and relational databases, it is very important to recognize that the object-oriented approach deals with data at a much higher level than a relational database. Whereas a relational database deals with data at the level of columns and rows, an object-oriented system deals with objects. An object may be an order, an inventory list, or any real-world representation of a physical object. For example, consider an object called ORDER. ORDER is a logical object to the object-oriented system, and each ORDER will have associated data items and behaviors. Behaviors might include PLACE_ORDER, CHANGE_ORDER, and so on.

At the relational database level, an ORDER is really a consolidation of many different columns from many different tables. The customer name comes from the CUSTOMER table, order date comes from the ORDER table, quantity from the LINE_ITEM table, and item description from the ITEM table. Hence, a single behavior for an object may cause changes to many tables within the relational database.

Many people have suggested the use of relational "views" to represent this higher level of abstraction. For example, an SQL statement could create a view called PLACE_ORDER, and this view could be embedded into a C++ program:

```
DEFINE DISPLAY_ORDER as
     Select CUST_NAME, CUST_ADDR,
             ORDER_NBR, ORDER_DATE, ITEM_DESC, QTY
     From  CUSTOMER, ORDER, LINE_ITEM, ITEM
     Where
             CUSTOMER.CUST_NBR = ORDER.CUST_NBR and
             ORDER.ORDER_NBR = LINE_ITEM.ORDER_NBR and
             LINE_ITEM.ITEM_NBR = ITEM.ITEM.NBR;
```

The view could then be used to produce an order listing in a single SQL statement:

```
SELECT * FROM DISPLAY_ORDER WHERE ORDER_NBR = 123;
```

This is an excellent approach for retrievals, but views cannot be used for update operations. In a relational view, the row ID (the RID) cannot be maintained within the subordinate tables, and consequently, UPDATE and INSERT operations are not allowed. Object behaviors such as PLACE_ORDER and CHANGE_ORDER cannot use relational views. Some researchers have suggested methods for creating "updatable" views within the relational database model (Scholl, 1990), but no commercial databases have implemented support for updatable views.

Another approach is to take the SQL and create methods for a C++ system:

```
void display_order(char* cust_name)
{
```

```
EXEC SQL BEGIN DECLARE SECTION;
CHAR mycust_name[20];
EXEC SQL END DECLARE SECTION;

mycust_name = cust_name

EXEC SQL
Select CUST_NAME, CUST_ADDR,
       ORDER_NBR, ORDER_DATE, ITEM_DESC, QTY
From   CUSTOMER, ORDER, LINE_ITEM, ITEM
Where
       CUSTOMER.CUST_NBR = ORDER.CUST_NBR and
       ORDER.ORDER_NBR = LINE_ITEM.ORDER_NBR and
       LINE_ITEM.ITEM_NBR = ITEM.ITEM.NBR and
       CUSTOMER.CUST_NAME = :mycust_name;
END-EXEC;
}
```

This use of methods within a C++ structure would also allow methods to be nested into a single call of the database. For example, the PLACE_ORDER behavior would become:

```
void place_order(char* cust_nbr, char* order_struct)
{
    check_credit(cust_nbr);
    check_inventory(order_struct);
    add_line_items(order_struct);
}
```

Each of the sub-behaviors would be called into the order specified in the PLACE_ORDER method, thereby maintaining the sequence for the data.

```
char check_credit(char* cust_nbr, int total_amt)
{
EXEC SQL BEGIN DECLARE SECTION;
int    mycust_nbr,
       credit_limit;
```

```
char myresult[3];
EXEC SQL END DECLARE SECTION

cust_nbr = cust_nbr;
EXEC SQL
SELECT CREDIT_LIMIT INTO :credit_limit
FROM CUSTOMER
WHERE CUST.CUST_NBR = :mycust_nbr;
END-EXEC;

if (credit_limit > total_amt)
{
        strcat(myresult, "AOK");
        return(0);
}
else
{
        strcat(myresult, "YUK");
        return(0);
}
}
```

7.3.   GENERALIZATION HIERARCHIES AND RELATIONAL DATABASES

Generalization hierarchies (the ISA relationship) are not supported by relational databases but are easily implemented by using separate tables, one for each subclass in the hierarchy. An ISA relationship is nothing more than a successive refinement of an entity, in which the general data items are physically separated from the specific detailed data items. For example, a database containing information about employees might create a hierarchy that would include information about the specific categories of employees.

Note that each data item within the class is unique to that class. A nonexempt employee has the data items of Wage and Overtime_rate, but also inherits the data items Employee_ID from the EMPLOYEE class, and Name and Sex from the PERSON

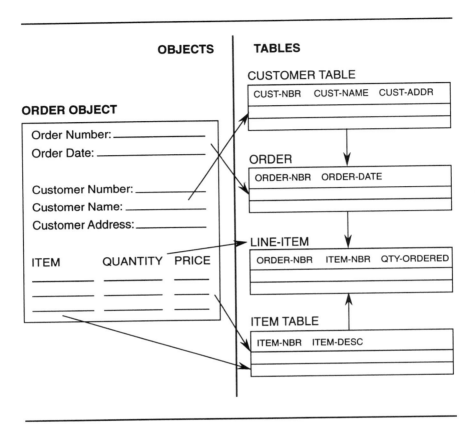

Figure 7.1. "Objects" and relational tables.

class. By using database triggers, the behaviors and the data attributes may be inherited, just as if the relational database were an object-oriented database.

The relational tables definitions to support this person class hierarchy could be implemented as follows:

```
ADD TABLE PERSON (
       PERSON_NAME                          CHAR(40),
       PERSON_SEX                           CHAR(1))
```

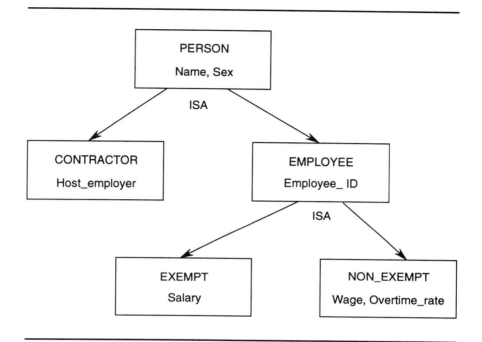

Figure 7.2. Employee class hierarchy.

```
ADD TABLE CONTRACTOR (
    PERSON_NAME REFERENCES PERSON.PERSON_NAME   CHAR(40),
    HOST_COMPANY                                CHAR(40))

ADD TABLE EMPLOYEE (
    PERSON_NAME REFERENCES PERSON.PERSON_NAME   CHAR(40),
    EMPLOYEE_ID                                 INTEGER))

ADD TABLE SALARIED (
    EMPLOYEE_ID REFERENCES EMPLOYEE.EMPLOYEE_ID INTEGER,
    SALARY                                      LONGINT))

ADD TABLE HOURLY (
    EMPLOYEE_ID REFERENCES EMPLOYEE.EMPLOYEE_ID INTEGER,
```

```
        WAGE                                      SMALLINT
        OVERTIME_RATE                             SMALLINT))
```

Under a relational database that supports triggers, a trigger would be defined for each of the lower-level tables, which would be fired before an action would take place. For example, assume that we have the following behaviors associated with the PEOPLE hierarchy:

1. HIRE person
2. CHANGE_PAYRATE for person

In the HIRE behavior, a trigger would be fired before the IN-SERT of a PERSON row. This trigger would INSERT the proper field values into the subordinate tables:

```
Create trigger HIRE_PERSON
        BEFORE INSERT OF PERSON

IF PERSON_TYPE = 'EMPLOYEE'
DO

        IF PERSON_TYPE = 'HOURLY'
            INSERT INTO HOURLY VALUES (EMP_ID, WAGE_RATE)

        IF PERSON_TYPE = 'SALARIED'
            INSERT INTO SALARY VALUES (EMP_ID, WAGE_RATE)

        INSERT INTO EMPLOYEE VALUES (PERSON_NAME, EMP_ID)

ELSE

        INSERT INTO CONTRACTOR
        VALUES ('PERSON_NAME, HOST_COMPANY)

ENDIF
```

Assume that the CHANGE_PAYRATE behavior uses a percentage rate for the pay rate change. Because two database tables contain pay information, the SALARY and the HOURLY tables, triggers must be written to fire after an update is performed against either of these columns.

```
Create Trigger CHANGE_PAYRATE
        BEFORE UPDATE OF HOURLY.WAGE
        WAGE = WAGE * PERCENTAGE
```

```
Create Trigger CHANGE_PAYRATE
        BEFORE UPDATE OF SALARY.WAGE
        SALARY = SALARY * PERCENTAGE
```

7.4. RECURSION AND RELATIONAL DATABASES

The recursive, or bill-of-materials, relationship is used whenever a class (or entity) has a many-to-many relationship with other objects in the system.

Consider for example, a behavior called COMPUTE_PROFIT that is required to recursively cascade through many levels of ITEM records in order to complete. The data relationship would look like a standard recursive relationship.

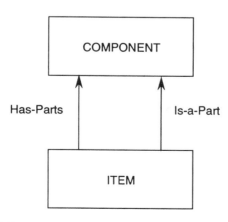

Figure 7.3. Item bill-of-material.

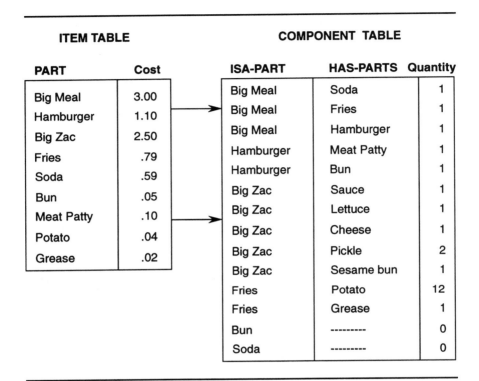

Figure 7.4.   Recursive relational tables.

The relational implementation of this construct requires that a junction table be created to establish the relationships for each component. To use Guttbaum's hamburger stand, this table structure might look like Figure 7.4.

The Component table has multiple entries, one for each component within an assembly, and we see that the Big Meal has three entries, one each for the soda, the fries, and the hamburger. In order to make a relational database function on a recursive SQL call, it is necessary to include those items that do not have any subassemblies, and this is why the Bun and Soda items appear in the component table, even though they do not have any subcomponents.

In order to properly cascade through the relational tables, the

SQL must be constructed so that the component table is joined against itself.

To calculate the profit for each item in the Item table, a view could be written in SQL:

```
Define GET_PROFIT as
Select distinct ITEM.ITEM, SUM(COST), ITEM.COST,
   ITEM.COST-SUM(COST)
      From ITEM A, COMPONENT B, COMPONENT C
      where A.ITEM = B.ITEM and
            B.ITEM = C.ITEM;
```

This is a very interesting application of SQL. Note that the table is joined with itself. This type of "self joining" tells the SQL to recursively descend the hierarchy.

Now that the SQL view is defined, it becomes simple to calculate the profit for an item by invoking the view:

```
SELECT * FROM GET_PROFIT WHERE ITEM = "Big Meal";
```

The resulting table would look like:

Big Meal	3.00	1.45	1.55
Hamburger	1.10	.15	.95
Fries	.75	.06	.69
Soda	.60	.07	.57
Meat Patty	.10	——	——
Bun	.05	——	——
Potato	.04	——	——
Grease	.02	——	——

As you can see, this report give a full breakdown of all of the components in a Big Meal, and a breakdown of all of the components within the components. These techniques are very useful for the design of object-oriented systems that must traverse these types of relationships.

7.5. SQL AND OBJECT-ORIENTED DATA MANIPULATION LANGUAGE

Another great benefit of the relational model was the introduction of Structured Query Language (SQL). SQL was a tremendous benefit because it removed the requirement of the database that the user of the system "navigate" the data structures. SQL is called "declarative" in the sense that the user need only specify the desired data, and the database engine will take care of the navigation. Hierarchical, network, and object-oriented databases require the programmers to navigate the data structures to get their selected data. With SQL the age of enduser access became a reality and users began to use SQL to access their information without programmer intervention.

The relational model uses SQL. SQL is a high-level, declarative language in which the user would simply state the desired constraints for the data, and leave the access method to a "database optimizer." "Declarative," in this context, means that the actual navigation path to the data is hidden from the user, and the user "declares" a solution set that meets the user's selection criteria. The SQL optimizer would determine the proper access for the data and handle all of the database navigation. For example, a database request for an order could be phrased:

```
SELECT CUST-ID, ORDER-NO
    FROM CUSTOMER, ORDER
    WHERE CUSTOMER.CUST-ID = ORDER.CUST-ID
    AND CUSTOMER.CUST-ID = 'IBM'
```

While it is impossible to describe every possible factor for the choice of database access languages, there are several general rules that may be applied to any query.

1. DML—Navigational, record-at-a-time processing

—Useful for maintenance of currency
—High-speed record retrieval
—Generally more resource-efficient than SQL
—Usually less productive for programmers

2. SQL—Declarative, "state space" processing

—Very productive for programmers, especially for complex requests
—Less efficient than navigational DML
—Database navigation paths are transparent
—All columns meeting matching criteria are displayed

DML and SQL are identical in function; both serve to retrieve data from the database. The real difference is the tradeoff between computer resource consumption and programmer productivity. A proficient SQL programmer can always outperform a proficient DML programmer, and in many cases SQL can be hundreds of times more productive than DML. However, the downside to SQL is the resource consumption and the need to reassemble objects from their component tables. Properly tuned SQL can perform competitively with DML, but poorly tuned SQL queries (especially correlated subqueries and nested queries) can create havoc on a relational system.

Before discussing the differences between SQL and DML it is best to first explore the similarities. For simple record-at-a-time access, SQL and DML are very similar:

SQL	DML
SELECT * FROM CUSTOMER	MOVE 'DON' TO CNAME.
WHERE CNAME = 'DON';	OBTAIN CALC CUSTOMER.

The most important conceptual difference between SQL and DML is the ability of SQL to "declare" the conditions that govern queries and updates. For example, suppose that you wanted to give a 10% raise to all salespeople who have sold more than $100,000 this year. In SQL this query would be simply:

```
UPDATE SALESPERSON SET SAL = SAL + (1. * SAL) WHERE SALES
> 100000;
```

Here is an example of an instance where a single SQL statement has replaced a DML program that would require many lines of code.

A real comparison between SQL and DML is rather difficult because of the syntactical and operational differences between the languages. Other than the fact that they both retrieve and update database information, there is very little similarity between the languages. DML programmers who are used to traditional navigation will be somewhat disconcerted by the lack of physical constructs in the SQL language. In fact, SQL only requires that the user know the name of the data item and the tables in which the item resides.

BEWARE: Declarative languages such as SQL often make assumptions on your behalf about the "intention" of your queries or updates. Consequently, it is not uncommon to receive a solution set from your SQL query that bears little resemblance to your intent.

7.6. SQL COMPARED TO CODASYL DML

Consider a salesperson database where a single record contains:

```
SALES-MONTH, SALES-YEAR, SALES-NAME, SALES AMOUNT
```

Let's assume that you wish to identify people who have sold more than 10% above their figures for the same month in the prior year.

In CODASYL DML:

```
MOVE 1990 TO YEAR.
OBTAIN FIRST SALESPERSON WITHIN SALES-IX.

WHILE ERROR-STATUS NE 0307
REPEAT.
      SAVE HOLD-KEY FROM SALESPERSON NEXT CURRENCY.
      ADD 1 TO SALES-YEAR.
      OBTAIN SALESPERSON WITHIN SALES-IX USING SALES-KEY.
      IF SALES-AMOUNT > .1 * HOLD-AMOUNT
            DISPLAY TEXT SALES-PERSON.
```

```
    OBTAIN NEXT SALESPERSON DB-KEY HOLD-KEY.
END.
```

In SQL:

```
SELECT A.SALES-PERSON
FROM SALES A, SALES B
WHERE
    A.MONTH = B.MONTH
    AND
    A.YEAR = 1990
    AND
    B.YEAR = 1991
    AND
    A. SALES_AMOUNT > .1 * B.SALES.AMOUNT;
```

7.7. PROBLEMS WITH RELATIONAL DATABASES AND OBJECT-ORIENTED TECHNIQUES

7.7.1. Currency

One major drawback of relational databases is their requirement that rows be addressed by the contents of their data values (usually the primary key). Object-oriented database models require the concept of "currency" so that records may be addressed independently of their data. The CODASYL model supports the declaration of abstract "sets" to relate classes together, and also supports the notion of "currency" whereby a record may be used without any reference to the record's data. SQL programmers have often lamented that it is sometimes difficult to determine where they are in the database when performing a complex operation. To be able to reference a row as "Current of Table" would be a tremendous addition to the SQL language.

7.7.2. Hidden Access Paths

Any object-oriented DML programmer is required to clearly describe the access path that the database will use to service the request. The access path is clearly described in the code, and the programmer can graphically show the path with a data-structure diagram (the Bachman diagram). In SQL however, the access path in not evident and is hidden within the SQL optimizer. The SQL optimizer interrogates the system tables to see if the "target" relational tables have indexes, then determines the optimal access path to service the SQL request. The SQL optimizer uses several access methods, including sequential scans, sequential pre-fetch, and index scans. Only by running the SQL EXPLAIN utility can the programmer see the access path to the data.

7.7.3. Inefficient SQL Statements

In many large or complex SQL queries there are numerous formats for the SQL statement that will give identical results. Unfortunately, many of these queries are vastly different in terms of access paths and resource consumption. For example, consider the request to compare two rows in the same table and to compute the difference between two amounts:

```
SELECT A.AMOUNT , B.AMOUNT
FROM CUST A
WHERE EXISTS
(SELECT * FROM CUST B WHERE B.DATE = 1091 AND A.DATE =
  0991)
```

This query will access the entire database for each instance on the outer select. If there were 100 rows in this table, the query would access row1 and then execute the subquery 100 times to satisfy the request. Therefore, this request would require 10,000 row retrievals.

The same query can be rewritten to avoid the nested subquery and dramatically reduce the amount of database access:

```
SELECT A.AMOUNT , B.AMOUNT
FROM CUST A , CUST B
WHERE
B.DATE = 1091 AND
A.DATE = 0991 AND
A.CNAME = B.CNAME
```

This query will only do one select and one join operation to produce the desired result.

7.8.   IMPEDANCE MISMATCHES AND RELATIONAL DATABASES

There is another problem encountered when using SQL with a general-purpose object-oriented programming language in which an "impedance mismatch" is created (Ahmed, 1992).
Ahmed states:

> *There are two aspects to this mismatch: (1) Difference in programming paradigms, for example, between a declarative language such as SQL and an imperative language such as C; and (2) a mismatch in the type systems, whereby loss of information occurs at the interface. In most relational systems, the DML* lacks computational completeness *to express complex mathematical manipulations of data common to engineering design. Most OODBMSs, on the other hand, provide database extensions to* computationally complete *programming languages (e.g., C++, CLOS, Smalltalk) that may be capable of handling complexities typical of large-scale programs such as finite element analysis.*

Rather than the term impedance mismatch, perhaps this phenomenon should be called a "paradigm mismatch." The relational and object-oriented methods are so vastly different in approach that these types of problems are bound to occur.

7.9.   PROBLEMS WITH AD HOC QUERY

There are several constructs within the SQL language that conflict with object-oriented databases. The most obvious is the requirement that SQL serve as an ad hoc query facility.

One of the basic constructs of object-oriented programming is encapsulation. Encapsulation is defined as the ability to access objects only via their behaviors. This is contradictory to a basic principle of the relational database model, data independence, which says that any data may be accessed in an ad hoc, independent fashion.

At first glance, it seems that these two concepts cannot be

reconciled, because it would be impossible to have data tables that are independent of the application while at the same time supporting encapsulation, which tightly couples the objects and their behaviors. However, these concepts are not contradictory. Because the behaviors are stored in the database, they are not external and will not jeopardize the independence of applications from data.

For example, one could only access the CREDIT_RATING field in the CUSTOMER table by invoking the PLACE_ORDER behavior. The SQL language, of course, would allow access and update to any data items that are allowed within the system security tables. Any authorized user could view the credit rating of a customer without ever invoking an object-oriented behavior.

Another problem relates to the SQL CREATE TABLE statement. Object-oriented systems allow the concept of abstract data typing, and programmers may create their own data types, which become indistinguishable from the system-defined data types. For example, an object-oriented programmer could define a data type of BOOLEAN, which would be treated by the system just like a CHAR or INTEGER data type. Relational technology does not have a facility for self-defining new data types, but I do not think that this is a problem, because the existing data types are acceptable for 99% of all systems.

Another conceptual limitation of SQL that has legitimate ramifications for object-oriented databases is the inability of SQL to associate a behavior with a data item. The properties of an object and its operational semantics must be coded within an external entity (the application program), and SQL has no built-in method for incorporating behaviors into tables. However, there is a solution to this problem.

Just as the DB2 database stores SQL statement in tables (the SYSSTATEMENT table), users of an interpretive database may create tables that can store predefined SQL statements and access them at runtime with dynamic SQL. This dynamic approach is somewhat like the object-oriented principle of "late binding," but it places a performance problem on the system. Rather than having all operations precompiled (i.e., optimized and ready to execute), the SQL optimizer must be invoked at every SQL statement.

Because the concepts of encapsulation and SQL are contradictory, does this mean that SQL may never be appropriate for use in OODBMS? I think not. The concept of encapsulation was created to achieve "data hiding" and to ensure that the object-oriented system maintains its own internal integrity. Databases have other mechanisms for maintaining security.

7.10. REFERENTIAL INTEGRITY AND OBJECT-ORIENTED CONSTRUCTS

The relational principle of referential integrity can be extended to help with the management of objects within an object-oriented database. Referential integrity is generally used to enforce relationships between two tables such that an "owner" row may not be deleted if member rows exist. This same principle could be applied to a relational implementation of an object-oriented database to ensure that all components of an object will coexist.

Consider an object called ORDER, which consists of one row in the ORDER table and several rows in the LINE_ITEM and ITEM tables.

ORDER FORM

Order Number_____   Order Date_____
Customer Name _____

ITEM DESCRIPTION	ITEM COST	QUANTITY ORDERED
_____	_____	_____
_____	_____	_____
_____	_____	_____

Because the ORDER object is a consolidation of rows from different tables, referential integrity could be used to ensure that the ORDER object maintains all of its components. The rules are as follows.

1. Ensure that the ITEM-ID row cannot be changed or deleted if the item participates in an order:

```
ALTER TABLE LINE_ITEM
ITEM-ID REFERENCES ITEM.ITEM_ID ON DELETE RESTRICT;
```

2. Ensure that the ORDER_NBR cannot be changed or deleted if the order has items attached:

```
ALTER TABLE LINE_ITEM
ORDER_NBR REFERENCES ORDER.ORDER_NBR ON DELETE
   RESTRICT;
```

This application of referential integrity ensures that an order always remains intact, and that any SQL statements will not inadvertently corrupt the integrity of an ORDER object.

7.11. VIEWS AND OBJECT-ORIENTED CONSTRUCTS

Views refer to the ability of the database to associate a single database command with a name, and then to treat the view name as if it were a single table. Under the concept of views, a large conglomeration of related tables may be combined into a single view, which can be addressed in subsequent SQL commands as if it were a table.

For example, a query that displays the names of all items and customers may be defined as:

```
DEFINE VIEW orderitem AS
SELECT ITEM_NAME, CUSTOMER_NAME
    FROM ITEM I, LINE_ITEM L, ORDER O, CUSTOMER C
    WHERE
    I.ITEM.NBR = L.ITEM_NBR AND
    L.ORDER_NBR = O.ORDER_NBR
    O.CUST_NBR = C.CUST_NBR
```

This new view, orderitem, may now be called as if it were a single relational table, greatly simplifying the query. To see the item names for a customer—say, IBM—one only needs to enter:

```
SELECT * FROM orderitem WHERE CUST_ID = "IBM"
```

The obvious problems with views is their inability to handle update operations. In a view, the specific row IDs (RIDs), are hidden from the application, making updates impossible. Relational databases are unable to keep track of row IDs when tables are joined.

Several researchers have attempted to define methods whereby updatable views may be incorporated into an object-oriented system, most notably the COCOON object data model (Scholl, 1990). In this paper, Scholl describes extensions to a relational language that allow a relational view to update relational tables. This same approach could be implemented to allow object-oriented control of relational tables. The SQL++ product from Oracle Corporation seems to have the best framework, but it remains to be seen if this product will offer complete control of a relational database at the object level.

PROBLEMS AND EXERCISES

1. Sketch an E/R model and a relational view to describe the following objects:

   A. An application for employment at ABC Corporation consists of a complete history of the applicant. The applicant will enter the standard biographical information, and will also be asked about each prior job. Educational history will also be gathered, and a self-assessment of job skills will also be included on the application form.

   B. An auto insurance claim form contains the following information. The name of the insured person is entered along with the name of the person who is making the claim. In addition, the form contains a complete description of the auto accident, including a description of the damage to each vehicle.

2. Use any commercial database system (DB2, Oracle, Ingres) to take a look at the structure of the system tables. How could these system tables be extended to incorporate objects and

classes? Give specific referential integrity rules for how your new tables could relate to the existing tables.

REFERENCES

Ahmed, S., Wong, A., Sriram, D., Logcher, R., "A comparison of object-oriented database management systems for engineering applications," MIT Technical Report IESL-90-03, 1990.

Babcock, C., "Object Lessons," *Computerworld*, May 3, 1993.

Burleson, D., "SQL generators," *Database Programming & Design*, July 1993.

De Troyer, O., Keustermans, J., Meersman, R., "How helpful is object-oriented language for an object-oriented database model?," International Workshop on Object-Oriented Database Systems, Proceedings, Wash., DC, IEEE Computer Society Press, 1986.

Loomis, M., "Integrating objects with relational technology," *Object Magazine*, July/August 1991.

Loomis, M., "Object and relational technology. Can they cooperate?," *Object Magazine*, July/August 1991.

McFadden, F., "Conceptual Design of object-oriented databases," *Journal of Object-Oriented Programming*, Vol. 4, Sept. 1991.

Scholl, M., Laasch, C., Tresch, M., "Updateable views in object-oriented databases," International Workshop on Object-Oriented Database Systems, Proceedings, Wash., DC, IEEE Computer Society Press, 1990.

Stone, C., "The rise of object databases: can the Object Management Group get database vendors to agree on object standards?," *DBMS*, July 1992.

Vasan, R., "Relational databases and objects: a hybrid solution," *Object Magazine*, July/August 1991.

Yourdon, E., "The marriage of relational and object-oriented design," *Relational Journal*, Vol. 3, Issue 6, Jan. 1992.

Distributed Object Technology: The New Generation of Distributed Software

8.1. INTRODUCTION

There has been an increasing need within the computer industry to effectively manage distributed computing systems. Thousands of companies, from small engineering firms to multi-billion dollar conglomerates, now have their mission-critical information on more than one computer. Distributed computing, by its very nature, is inherently complex, and methods must be devised to control the interfacing between the hardware platforms. Object-oriented technology offers a solution. Independent objects can be created to manage all of the complexities of client-server and distributed processing, allowing the user to freely connect and exchange information across widely diverse hardware and software systems.

The general trend of the 1990s has been to move away from the cumbersome mainframe computers into a distributed network of processing, often with client-server technology. The term *client-server* is used to describe the interaction between data repositories and applications. The data may be a centralized database on an IBM mainframe, a distributed database on a set of minicomputers, a PC network, or any combination of platforms. The server resides on the same platform as the data, and interacts, via a network, to retrieve and update data. The distributed nature of these types of systems has a tremendous impact on the future of object technology. In order for an object-oriented application to function in a distributed environment, a standardized set of interfaces must be established. These interfaces will ensure that all requests for objects will adhere to a standard protocol.

8.2.   HISTORICAL BACKGROUND

In the early 1960s, corporations began to change their attitudes about information. Prior to this time, corporate information was considered a burden, a thing to be managed and controlled. However, the widespread availibility of commercial database management caused corporations to rethink their attitude about information. Corporations began to consider their information to be an asset, an asset that could be exploited to make better and faster decisions. As most companies adopted database systems, reaction time to changes in the marketplace dropped significantly, and companies had to be able to consult their databases quickly to stay ahead of their competition. By the 1970s, corporate databases were firmly entrenched, and companies struggled to collect and disseminate their information.

One of the main goals of database management systems was the concept of the "central repository," which would store all of the corporation's information and allow information to be accessed and distributed to all areas of the corporation. Many companies underwent expensive conversion efforts and established mega-databases that contained many gigabytes of corporate information. The centralized repository promised to allow complete control and sharing of information for all areas within the organization.

As the idea of the corporate repository matured, companies discovered that many of the promises of database technology were not being fulfilled. Even though the data was stored in a central repository, the managers complained that some information was not being provided to them, or the information was not in a form that the managers could use. Many within the company also felt that they were hostages to their information systems department. In order to make changes to their systems, they were forced to

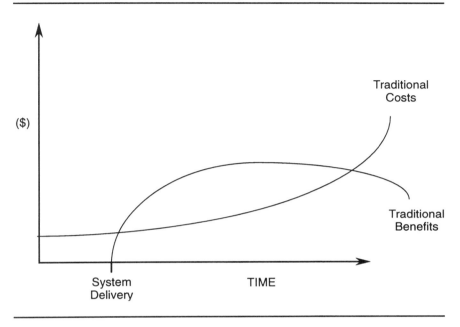

Figure 8.1. Traditional systems eventually become too cumbersome to maintain.

work with a team of programmers who they felt were unresponsive to their needs. Simple changes could often take many months and cost thousands of dollars.

The promise of perpetual systems also proved to be a fallacy. Systems designed to have a useful life of several decades were literally falling apart as a result of constant maintenance. Systems that were delivered with complete documentation and well-structured code became unmanageable conglomerations of "spaghetti" that were very hard to maintain. An excellent example was the Social Security system. When it was first delivered, the programs were well-structured and completely documented, and processed hundreds of thousands of Social Security checks each month. This very same system received Senator Proxmire's "Golden Fleece" award several years later, when the system was paying Social Security benefits to many people who were not entitled to benefits. The system, once pristine and well-structured, had become so unmanageable that even the programming staff had trouble describing the functions of each program. The system had to be scrapped and redesigned.

Even with centralized databases, users were still faced with the problem of diverse data platforms. Many companies embarked on "downsizing" or "rightsizing" their system to take advantage of the cheaper processing of minicomputers and PC platforms. In the process, many users abandoned the idea of a central repository of data, and attempted to build "bridges" between the applications. Unfortunately, these bridges were often quite complex and difficult to manage. For example, establishing communications between a PC relational database and a CODASYL mainframe database is very cumbersome.

Many companies found that the frequent reorganizations and corporate acquisition led to many diverse platforms for their information. Most large companies have many different database management systems, and perhaps dozens of hardware platforms. These market conditions have led many information systems managers to develop systems in a reactive mode, focusing on the immediate need for these systems to communicate rather than on a common, centralized access method.

In the 1980s, IBM introduced the concept of enterprise modeling, whereby the entire organization's information was modeled, and the overall system was composed of a large client-server environment. This model was based on the idea that data should become independent of its source, and that information can be accessed regardless of the type of database manager and hardware platform.

Today, many companies adopt the posture that their systems should exploit the "right" database systems, and it is acceptable to have many different database systems on many different platforms. A marketing system, for example, is ideal for a relational database, while a CAD system is well-suited for an object-oriented database.

Friendly application interfaces also helped to foster downsizing. As endusers were exposed to windowing systems on PC networks, they began to view the block-mode systems on the mainframe as unacceptable, and began to be more demanding on the information systems staff to produce systems that were friendlier and more intuitive.

The goal of a centralized data repository could never materialize, especially for dynamic companies. Acquisitions of new companies, mergers, and reorganizations ensured that the manager was always faced with diverse information systems, each on its own platform with widely different software. Ironically, the reasons for many acquisitions of new companies was to take advantage of the synergy that would materialize from the sharing of information between the companies. Consequently, the information systems manager became the agent to achieve this synergy and was faced with the complex problem of establishing communications between the diverse platforms.

8.3. BASICS OF CLIENT-SERVER SYSTEMS

In the mainframe environments of the 1960s and 1970s, most online computer systems were characterized by "dumb terminals" that connected to a single data system. The terminal provided the user interface, while the application logic and database access were controlled by the mainframe.

Client-server, at its most basic, refers to the ability of a client, or requester, to make a request for services to another computer. The computer that receives the request, the server, interprets the request, and accesses the appropriate database, shipping the data as a response to the client.

Unlike the mainframe environment, client-server architectures allow the application code to reside in the client environment. By having the application code tightly coupled with the user's environment, the user is free to manipulate information using any tool within his or her environment, and to request data access services from many databases on other computer systems.

As many companies began to downsize their systems to take advantage of the cheaper processors on smaller platforms, early client-server systems were developed to manage information across many diverse platforms.

Three terms came into vogue at this time; front-end, back-end, and middleware. Middleware is the term used to describe the software that establishes an application programming inter-

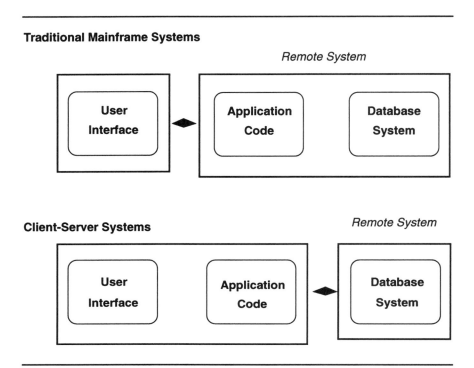

Figure 8.2.   Client-server moves the application into the user environment.

face, or API, for distributed applications. Front-end software refers to the client, which sends requests for services, and the back-end generally refers to the server, which receives and processes the request. In truly distributed processing, these terms are dynamic, because a front-end for any transaction may also be the back-end for another transaction.

8.4.   FRONT-END SOFTWARE

Generally, front-end software falls into two categories.

1. **Reporting and query tools** These systems provide one-way data transmission from the database server to the client. Because these systems are retrieval only, the sophistication

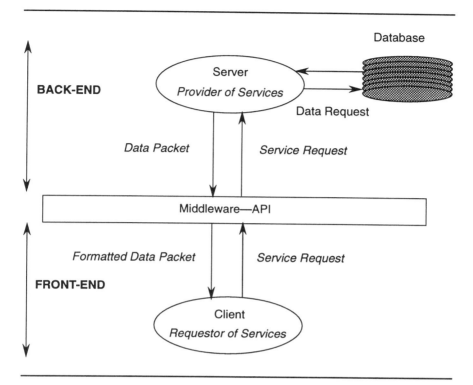

Figure 8.3.   Client-server architecture.

underlying the data requests is hidden from the user. Examples of this type of software include "Quest"® by Gupta™ corporation and the Oracle® database server. These tools allow the user to specify information requests in a friendly manner, such as building a sample report or specifying the desired information for a graph. The front-end then interrogates the request and generates SQL, which is sent to the server for processing. The requested information is delivered to the user and is formatted into the desired form, providing the user with spreadsheets and graphics.

2. **Program development software** Most packages that are offered on multiple platforms fall into this category. These types of systems allow the programmer to develop a system

on the PC and access information from a robust database server, such as DB2 on the mainframe, or Oracle on a UNIX system. These products include Gupta's SQLWindows and Microsoft's Visual Basic, as well as some of the new graphical user interface (GUI) tools for PCs.

GUI tools (pronounced "gooey") are among the hottest tools in client-server development software, and many of these tools promise to use object-oriented methods. Objectview® tools from Matesys, SQLWindows® Version 4.0, and Powersoft's PowerBuilder® are examples of object-oriented GUI tools.

Presentation managers are excellent examples of front-end software. Tools such as Microsoft Windows® handle all of the processing on the client, such as mouse clicks and window scrolling. Requests are passed to a data manager, which passes the request to the API for processing on the host server. Many of the most sophisticated of these tools, such as Powersoft's PowerBuilder, manage all of the Windows and SQL formatting, leaving the user to develop an application without concern for the internals of the presentation manager or the workings of the data structures.

There are three levels of front-end client-server. The simplest is a presentation manager on the client, with all of the presentation logic and data access logic on the server. Other configurations may have the presentation manager and presentation logic on the client, with the data access logic on the server. Another has the presentation manager, presentation logic, and the data logic on the client.

8.5. BACK-END SOFTWARE

Back-end software is the software that manages requests from the client and retrieves the information from the database server, and passes it to the client front-end. Most of these products only serve a single type of client, although multiple database back-ends can be installed on a single data repository.

In most client-server environments, the server is a single database that interacts with the client. In distributed database environments, a back-end may be a distributed database manager that manages multiple requests against many databases, collect-

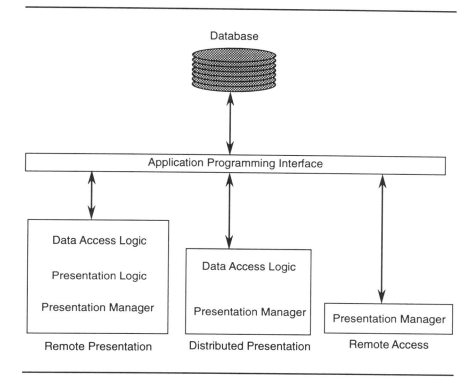

Figure 8.4. Three types of client front-ends.

ing and formatting the requested information into a single packet for the client. A distributed database manager may deal with information that is in many different physical locations, and the manager maps this diverse data into a single logical package. So far as the client is concerned, the server is a single, logical database engine.

The back-end software interprets the request from the client and determines the physical access path to retrieve the desired data. The back-end system is also responsible for all database interface and includes all database logic for rollback, error handling, and database commit processes. Because the back-end software is the only entity dealing directly with the database, the back-end is responsible for maintaining all transactions from the client.

Middleware is the interface layer between the client and the server. However, middleware is going out of vogue as a buzzword because of a recent decision by the US Patent and Trademark Office. They have granted a registered trademark on the term "Middleware™" to the software firm of TechGnosis™ Inc. The trademark was granted on the basis of their early use of the term, and TechGnosis now has exclusive rights to the word Middleware.

Client-server software usually uses an application programming interface (API), a request language (SQL), and a local and remote "service layer" to manage the interaction between the platforms.

Client-server software can be divided into five major areas, which include file transfer software, messaging products with both an API and communications services for distributed networks, database/data access packages that link to various databases, online transaction processing systems, and remote procedure calls with an API that works over multiple protocol stacks.

8.6.   DISTRIBUTED OBJECT-ORIENTED TECHNOLOGY

There are many problems with client-server and distributed database systems that have influenced many corporations to postpone entry into this technology. The foremost reason for not using client-server technology is a fear of the complexity of the interfaces between the systems. "This technology will provide an evolutionary approach to the development of this much-needed solution," says Chris Stone, President of the Object Management Group. Corporations that have invested millions of dollars in their information systems tend to be very conservative, and while many have acknowledged that object technology is a great idea, they continue to wait until the technology is fully tested and widely accepted.

While object technology and distributed systems technology may seem to be very different in scope and purpose, they complement each other very nicely for the development of distributed systems. Object technology has been used successfully by numerous vendors to simplify client-server systems. Connection to a remote database has now become as simple as selecting and dragging an icon. All of the complex interactions between presentation managers and data managers are now hidden from the users and developers, and object-oriented application programming interfaces (APIs) are revolutionizing the way that people think about distributed systems.

Even though millions of people now have personal computers at their desks, most personal computers are vastly underutilized. For most nontechnical users, a PC is nothing more than a tool that is used for simple word processing or spreadsheet tasks. The users have neither the time nor the inclination to learn all of the technical details of a product and seldom take advantage of all of the advanced features. The introduction of object-oriented operating systems will tap into a huge market of users who want their software to do what they want without complexity. When functionality is encapsulated into objects, users will be able to assemble and combine objects, and many more users will enjoy more functionality in their everyday tasks.

Companies are also frustrated about having "mature" legacy systems, which require expensive programming staffs to support. The user community has been clamoring for a technology to create systems that do not decay over time, and systems that do not become unmanageable as a result of constant maintenance. Object-oriented methods promise to deliver systems with a perpetual lifespan, because maintenance of encapsulated code is easier and all side effects of a program change can be isolated and identified. Since object-oriented technology has gained market acceptance, vendors have begun to sell object libraries that contain all of the building blocks to create a myriad of new distributed networks. This nascent technology will see a wild surge in popularity as more and more companies discover the benefits of coupling object technology with distributed systems.

The Object Management Group has been very active in the establishment of standard interfaces for object-oriented distributed systems; their common object request broker architecture (CORBA) has been widely accepted, and vendors are developing distributed object technology tools that will revolutionize the software market in the 1990s. IBM, Hewlett-Packard, Digital Equipment Corporation®, and many others have recognized the huge market potential for object-oriented distributed systems.

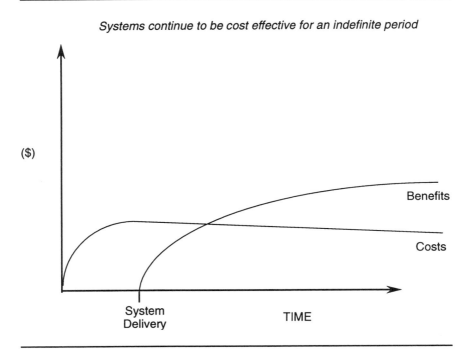

Figure 8.5.   Object-oriented systems.

Many LAN packages are now offering object-oriented interfaces. The new IBM product for OS/2 and Windows clients is called Thunderbird® Networking Software. Thunderbird serves as a "transport layer," allowing the user to select from a series of objects to create a LAN-to-WAN gateway. Users of Thunderbird can select an object, dial into a remote LAN, and behave just as if they were onsite. The popular Raima database server also offers an object-oriented GUI for establishing connections to SQL servers.

There are numerous projects to create object-oriented distributed systems to herald the introduction to this new architecture. Some of the major efforts include:

1. The Pink® system by Taligent™
2. NeXTSTEP® by NeXT®
3. BOCA® by Borland™

4. DSOM (OS/2)® by IBM
5. Cairo® (Windows NT) by Microsoft
6. DOMF® by Hewlett-Packard and SunSoft®
7. DOE® by SunSoft

Each of these products is described individually on the following pages. Because all of these products are currently under development, it is very difficult to accurately access the features of each product. The descriptions are based on vendor presentations and product announcements, and while some descriptions are vague, they provide a general overview of the direction of distributed object-oriented technology.

The players in this market will continue to jockey for position and align their products to capture market share. However, some vendors may be able to "force" their products on the market with massive marketing campaigns or by bundling their software with other system components. The good news for the user community is that each of the products will comply with the CORBA standard, and a new type of interoperability will become widely available.

8.6.1. Pink by Taligent Incorporated

In 1992, IBM and Apple Inc. entered a joint venture to develop a revolutionary object-oriented operating system. Apple had been developing their own object-oriented operating system, code-named the Pink project, and the joint venture established a new company, Taligent Inc. Taligent also is using the highly regarded micro-kernel product called Mach 3, which was developed at Carnegie-Mellon University. The Mach kernel will also be incorporated into later releases of OS/2 and AIX.

The 125 developers on the Pink project moved to Taligent, which now employs more than 250 developers. Taligent has formed three primary business groups. The Development Environment Group (DEG) is responsible for soliciting third-party vendors to develop tools, such as utilities, for Pink. The Native Systems Group (NSG) is working on versions of Pink for various hardware, including Intel and Motorola chips. The Complementary Products Group (CPG) will be a remarketing group and is developing standard class libraries for Pink.

Pink promises to be a complete operating environment and

toolset. It will have full object-oriented architecture and is being created from the hardware level, meaning that all system operations, including basic input and output, will be governed by the environment.

This bottom-up approach promises to make Pink a processor-independent and portable product. Conventional operating systems such as DOS are constrained by their own architectures, and even small enhancements to the base operating system are very hard to assimilate. By using an object-oriented framework, Pink hopes to be easily extensible and simple to enhance and reconfigure. The ability to adapt quickly to changes in technology could give Pink a major advantage in the marketplace.

Pink is being marketed as a "vertical" product, focusing on value-added resellers and developers who specialize in system integration. Taligent is totally committed to the object-oriented approach in their operating system, and they foresee that object technology will become a necessity for all operating systems in the future.

Numerous third-party vendors are already developing tools for Pink. Borland, Novell, and WordPerfect Corp. have all expressed support for Taligent's efforts, although there have been no product announcements as of May 1993. Pink is being developed in a secret environment, and few developers have seen the working code.

Backward compatibility is also an issue for Pink. Objects must be created for existing applications to run under the new object environment. Compatibility with existing file structures is critical to the success of Pink. No matter how revolutionary, the Pink system must be able to support legacy applications. One of the major problems with IBM's OS/2® is that it is not compatible with existing operating systems such as MS/DOS®. The inability of OS/2 to read MS/DOS files has been a primary reason for the slow acceptance of OS/2, even though OS/2 is considered to be technically superior to MS/DOS. IBM and Apple are currently working on software adapters that will allow Pink users to run existing Macintosh and OS/2 applications.

The greatest promise of Pink is the ability of developers to create cross-platform programs. This is very important to value-added resellers, who could use Pink to create custom systems that could be embedded in other system components. For example, a developer could use Pink objects to create a spreadsheet system that could be coupled with a database.

Parts of the Pink system will be appearing in IBM's OS/2 and AIX® systems in 1993. The incorporation of object-oriented layers into OS/2 should improve the overall functionality of OS/2, and will work with the System Object Model (SOM®). Pink will probably provide objects for dealing with system tasks such as graphics. Objects will allow OS/2 to be more portable, and even to run multiplatform applications. In theory, OS/2 could utilize the Pink objects to run simultaneously on a PC and UNIX. At this time, Apple has no plans to incorporate Pink code into their System 7 operating system.

Pink is competing with several other object-oriented operating systems developments, namely, NeXTSTEP® from NeXT, Inc. and Windows NT® (Cairo) from Microsoft. Pink is scheduled to ship in 1994 or 1995, after the scheduled delivery of Cairo.

8.6.2. NeXTSTEP from NeXT Computer Incorporated

NeXT Computer is promising to deliver a remarkable product for client-server development in an object-oriented environment. NeXTSTEP is an object-oriented operating system that is scheduled for delivery in the summer of 1993. Like Pink from Taligent Inc., NeXTSTEP is based on the Mach 3 micro-kernel from Carnegie Mellon University. NeXTSTEP has been shipping for some time, and recently a NeXTSTEP for Intel Processors was introduced. Next hopes to compete directly with other object-oriented operating systems offerings, namely Windows NT (Cairo) and Pink, neither of which will be introduced in 1993. With endusers having become accustomed to delays in delivery from software vendors, the early introduction of NeXTSTEP may prove to be a major market advantage, provided that NeXTSTEP is relatively bug-free and offers all of the promised functionality.

This PC-based client-server tool allows users to develop systems that communicate seamlessly by using objects, and includes a library of objects. For example, NeXTSTEP has a set of database objects that allow the user to connect to a database by choosing and dragging the desired database icon. The icon contains all of the code required to connect to the SQL server for the database. NeXTSTEP promises a complete object-oriented operating environment, with all of the robust features that are inherent in an object-oriented system.

NeXTSTEP has also announced a tool called Portable Distributed Objects (PDO®), which will enhance the client-server capabilities of their product. PDO allows systems running on client-server machines to access objects from high-speed network servers. PDO is expected to be generally available by the end of 1993.

8.6.3. The Borland Object Component Architecture (BOCA)

BOCA is the method Borland has chosen to integrate all of the products within the Borland family. In theory, BOCA will allow common communications between Paradox®, dBASE, C++, and Object PASCAL.

The framework for BOCA is the Borland Desktop. Desktop functions as an all-purpose environment and, similar to Microsoft Windows, acts as a container for "User Friendly Objects," or UFOs. Desktop claims to provide a complete object-oriented environment and allows the user to access and customize any object within the framework. For example, a user could enter the "object inspector" and review all of the data attributes and behaviors for a UFO. The data and behaviors could then be modified to dynamically create a new UFO. Example of UFOs are graphics interfaces, print managers, and all of the customizable screen icons, including push buttons, spinners, radio buttons, and data fields.

BOCA is designed to integrate all Borland tools, but it is only used within the context of a single workstation. Client-server and remote workstation connections are not directly supported by BOCA. These functions are delivered with Borland's Integrated Database API (IDAPI), which uses the Borland InterBase Engine. The InterBase Engine will also support remote database drivers and the "object layer." Borland is also developing the Borland Object Exchange Architecture (BOEX), which they hope will support remote data access. BOEX is still in the planning stages, but Borland hopes to extend their single-machine BOCA system to multiple platforms. BOEX is to be based on the BOCA architecture, and Borland would like the tools to be a fully functional peer-to-peer distributed architecture.

A delivery date for the IDAPI has not yet been set, and the detailed functionality of IDAPI has not been published. However, some assumptions can be made based on the promises from Borland. To truly integrate all Borland databases, the IDAPI must be able to access nonstandard SQL databases such as dBASE and Paradox, in addition to a standard SQL interface for relational databases. In fact, any "open" connectivity package will need to deal with nonSQL databases. The most reasonable approach to this problem is to have the tool create a logical request that could then be parsed into the appropriate access language for the database. Under this scenario, a request could be translated into the SQL dialect for Paradox, and into a record-oriented syntax for nonSQL databases. This "dual access" strategy has been successfully implemented in the CA-IDMS® database. CA-IDMS Release 12.0 supports both relational and network data architectures under a single database engine, and requests are translated into the appropriate syntax depending on the target database. Borland has announced that they will handle this dual access with virtual tables. A virtual table is a common view of a database table, and this common view may be composed of data from different databases. In order to join tables from different databases, the InterBase Engine must be able to join a relational table with a nonrelational table in a single query, and pass this data to the user by using a virtual table.

In order to compete with the huge Windows market, IDAPI also plans to establish bridges to allow Borland components to interface with Windows as well as with OS/2 and the AIX operating system. Conversely, Microsoft is now shipping its Open Database Connectivity (ODBC) product, which allows Windows applications to communicate with Borland products. Being "first to market" is critical to both Microsoft and Borland, because the company who delivers a truly open connectivity tool will enjoy a tremendous market advantage. Because the InterBase Engine is already a mature product on the UNIX platform, Borland has a much better chance of bringing the product to the marketplace faster than Microsoft.

The InterBase Engine uses a peer-to-peer architecture, which means that any instance of InterBase can serve as either a client or a server. For example, the InterBase Engine on a PC could be the client, while another instance of InterBase on UNIX could be the server.

Unlike the Microsoft Windows environment, Borland has chosen to implement object communications with Dynamic Link Libraries (DLLs). Because the DLLs are precompiled, the BOCA architecture runs far faster then Microsoft's Object Linking and Embedding (OLE), but it will not support dynamic binding of objects.

Borland has also introduced a visual programming tool for enduser development. The tool is called ObjectVision and allows the enduser to use "forms" to create screens and reports. ObjectVision is designed to run in a Windows shell and allows the endusers to create applications that access both relational databases and ASCII files. ObjectVision will access Paradox and dBASE databases on the PC, and will also allow client-server connections to Sybase and DB2. This means that, in theory, any enduser could create a Windows application that could access data from three platforms simultaneously, for example, accessing data from the PC, a UNIX database, and an IBM mainframe.

8.6.4. The Distributed Systems Object Model (DSOM) by IBM

IBM has made a commitment to object technology with their long-term plans for the OS/2 operating systems environment. The Distributed Systems Object Model® (DSOM) is scheduled for delivery in late 1993 and is an extension of the Systems Object Model® (SOM) which currently exists within IBM's OS/2® operating system. The Systems Object Model is designed to provide a language-independent method for defining class libraries and managing communications between objects, and DSOM adds a distributed component to this architecture.

Because DSOM will provide a language-independent and standard interface, IBM is currently working on compiler enhancements that will allow DSOM statements to be embedded within standard third-and fourth-generation languages. Other third-party compiler vendors have also committed to delivering languages that support SOM, including Borland's C++ and Microfocus COBOL. Digitalk Inc. has also announced support for SOM in its family of SmallTalk language products.

It is important to understand that SOM is a tightly integrated component of the OS/2 operating system and not just an implementation of an object-oriented operating system. In other words, the base object classes created within OS/2 become a part of the OS/2 system and are dynamically bound to programs at execution time. At runtime, SOM currently acts as an object-oriented messaging system whereby the sending object acts as a client, sending messages to the receiving object, which acts as a server. This type of architecture, combined with the language-independent feature, implies that DSOM will not require that the client and server software be written in the same language. As an object-oriented tool, SOM has some shortcomings, such as a lack of support for multiple inheritance; a new upgrade to SOM, SOM-2, is planned in order to address multiple inheritance and support for C++.

DSOM development is closely tied to the Taligent Inc. Pink system, and components from Pink are being incorporated into DSOM. Because IBM and Apple have undertaken a joint effort to create the Pink operating system, it is not clear whether OS/2 and Pink will be competitors or Pink will eventually replace OS/2. Regardless, DSOM and Pink will share a large portion of their base architecture. IBM has announced that all future releases of OS/2 will incorporate many of the object-oriented features of the Taligent product, and IBM also claims that Taligent is not a successor to OS/2. At this time, it is not clear how future releases of OS/2 will fare in the marketplace after the introduction of Pink, and IBM appears to be unwilling to abandon OS/2 in favor of the Taligent effort.

IBM has committed to implementing DSOM in accordance with the common object request broker architecture (CORBA) by the Object Management Group. This will ensure that DSOM systems will be compatible with other CORBA systems on different platforms.

IBM plans to incorporate DSOM into many different platforms, including midrange and mainframe systems, and IBM is currently collaborating with Novell Inc. to create a cross-platform system standard based on DSOM. This cross-platform standard will be called the Distributed Computing Environment (DCE). DCE is an environment for open systems that is currently in beta testing.

Many professional evaluators consider SOM to be more robust than other object-oriented development environments such as ObjectVision and Visual Basic, and the future implementation of DSOM will contain complete APIs, message systems, and database servers.

8.6.5. Cairo by Microsoft Incorporated

Cairo is the code word used to describe the next major release of Microsoft Windows NT operating system. Scheduled for delivery in 1994, Cairo claims to offer a fully distributed object-oriented operating system. While Microsoft has been very vague about the details of Cairo, some features can be inferred by examining the current release of Windows NT. Clearly, Microsoft intends to capitalize on their huge Windows market to become the dominant object-oriented development system for personal computers. The team leader for Cairo is James Allchin, who has a proven track record at Banyan Incorporated, where he developed a well-received distributed computer environment. Microsoft has announced that Cairo will also support multimedia and pen-based computing.

Cairo is being designed as a low-level operating system, with management of the system at the physical storage level and not up to the object level. In addition to the management of distributed tasks, Cairo will also manage system security and integrity. While Microsoft has not announced details about the database engine for this system, it will probably be an all-encompassing database manager with an object request broker for the front-end. Object management will probably take the form of an extended release of Object Linking and Embedding (OLE). OLE is used as an integration tool within most of the Microsoft product line and adopts a simplistic object-oriented method.

While Microsoft has not yet expressed a full commitment to support the CORBA standard for distributed object technology, Chris Stone, President of the Object Management Group, has stated that he expects Cairo to "closely" follow the CORBA standard. Regardless of the quality of Cairo, it is probably going to capture a large share of the distributed market, especially if the current releases of Windows NT are well-received.

8.6.6. Distributed Object Management Facility (DOMF) by Hewlett-Packard and SunSoft Incorporated

Hewlett-Packard (HP) made a commitment to the development of object-oriented technology with the creation of their Distributed Object Computing Program (DOCP), which will function as a superset of HP's Distributed Application Architecture (DAA).

In a very interesting turn of events, Hewlett-Packard entered into a joint effort with their major competitor, Sun Microsystems. In a joint submission to the Object Management Group (OMG), Sun and HP delivered the Distributed Object Management Facility (DOMF), which allows for the creation of distributed systems. DOMF will be fully compliant with the CORBA standard and includes a complete object broker that allows multiplatform systems development. HP has always been committed to development standards for object-oriented systems and was a founding member of the Object Management Group. HP and Sun hope that DOMF will allow users to take advantage of object-oriented distributed systems without having to adopt a new operating system.

The data storage engine behind DOMF will be the Hewlett-Packard database, OpenODB®. Unlike other object-oriented databases, OpenODB has support for relational architectures with its object-oriented structured query language (OSQL).

The HP efforts with DOCP will integrate many of the HP products, including OpenODB, HP Visual User Environment (HP-VUE®), and HP's version of C++, C++/SoftBench®, as well as the HP line of OpenView products. HP also plans to enhance the functionality of existing products by incorporating DOMF utilities. Especially important will be the enhancements to HP's NewWave®. NewWave Version 4 will be a distributed enhancement to allow the object-oriented facilities of NewWave to function in a distributed environment. Version 4 of NewWave also supports Microsoft's Windows DLLs and Microsoft's object linking and embedding (OLE) tool. Most users of NewWave Version 4 will probably choose to use the OLE API rather than the NewWave API, since HP has indicated that they plan to get out of the desktop API business.

The heart of DOMF is an object-oriented class definition facility and includes a location broker. The HP location broker governs the behavior of three key services:

1. The Manager of Object Region Experts (MORE®)
2. The Object Region Expert (ORE®)
3. The Manager of Objects Manager (MOM®)

The Manager of Objects Manager (MOM) stores information about several object managers, allowing distributed processing. MOM works with a Object Region Expert (ORE), which stores information about the storage domains for each MOM. At the highest level, the Manager of Object Region Experts (MORE) stores information about each MOM within the ORE.

HP and Sun are developing their own separate implementations of DOMF. Unfortunately, even though both implementations share a common architecture, Sun's DOMF will not handle naming conventions and binding in the same way as the HP version of DOMF.

8.6.7. Distributed Objects Everywhere (DOE®) by SunSoft Incorporated

SunSoft, the software development division of Sun Microsystems, has recently completed project DOE, an object-oriented distributed environment that is intended to compete with other vendors creating object-oriented distributed systems. As of June 1993, the project DOE development kit has been shipped to a small number of firms, and SunSoft intends to make the product available for general release by 1994. While it is not clear how DOE will work with Sun's version of DOMF, project DOE has contracted with Object Design Incorporated, the creators of the highly regarded ObjectStore database, to develop a Persistent Storage Manager Engine (PSME) to serve as the heart of DOE. PSME will use a subset of the ObjectStore database to allow DOE to store basic object information. Of course, DOE will comply with the CORBA standard.

8.7. PRODUCT SUMMARY

The commitment of the major vendors to develop object-oriented distributed environments indicates that distributed object technology is not a "flash in the pan." DOT will become an integral part of all new operating systems, and with the growing desire for client-server architectures it seems clear that object-oriented technology will become ingrained in mainstream systems development in the late 1990s.

With all of the simultaneous development, it is apparent that each of the offerings will attempt to carve out the largest market share. Being "first to market" is a very important part of market share, and many vendors will be tempted to release their DOT systems before they are fully debugged. It remains to be seen how the market will react to this new technology, but it is clear that all distributed operating systems will employ an object-oriented engine, and that systems developers must learn to employ the new technology.

The greatest threat to the vendors is the large promises of DOT as a panacea for all of the troubles of client-server computing. While object-oriented technology will clearly improve the usefulness and maintenance of client-server implementations, the initial development time may not live up to users' expectations. The next two years will be critical for the DOT vendors, and the fierce competition that is sure to result among the vendors will bode well for users. Competition always helps users, and the vendors will continue to scramble to improve their offerings.

When each is eventually introduced and evaluated, the marketplace will decide which environments will become dominant. Regardless of which operating system achieves market dominance, it is clear that object-oriented operating systems will become a major force in the next decade.

8.8. CORBA—A COMMON ARCHITECTURE FOR DISTRIBUTED SYSTEMS

Many organizations are recognizing the importance of standards in the emerging area of object-oriented systems development. In the spring of 1992, the Object Management Group (OMG), a nonprofit corporation dedicated to developing object standards, published the CORBA standard for object-oriented development. CORBA is the Common Object Request Broker Architecture, and was developed jointly by Sun, Hewlett-Packard, Digital Equipment Corp., NCR, and Hyperdesk Corporation. CORBA creates a standard protocol for an object to place requests and to receive responses from other objects. It is interesting to note that these competing vendors, who have a vested interest in proprietary software, have agreed to adhere to the CORBA standard in the development of new object-oriented systems.

Most of the major distributed operating systems have announced that they will adhere to the Common Object Request Broker Architecture (CORBA). Consequently, it is very important to understand the architecture that will become the foundation for distributed systems.

The balance of this chapter is selected text from the Object Management Architecture Guide (c) 1993, and is reproduced with the permission of the Object Management Group.

Chris Stone, the President and CEO of the Object Management Group, states:

> *The OMG's goal is to get everybody to agree on a messaging format and how objects talk to each other; get them to agree to the language and a model of how to structure the data; get them to agree to some common interfaces; get them to agree on how to do security and containment. . . . The real significance of the CORBA specification is for application developers who want to build new client-server applications that will work across disparate platforms.*

8.8.1. Introduction

As the 1980s twin business pressures of decentralization and globalization became apparent, technology again came to the rescue in the form of personal computers and desktop computing. All of the information about the running of a business, however, was distributed throughout the many computing resources of the business.

To make use of information effectively, it must be accurate and accessible across the department, even across the world. This means that the CPUs must be intimately linked to the networks of the world and be capable of freely passing and receiving information, not hidden behind glass and cooling ducts or the complexities of the software that drives them.

The major hurdles in entering this new world are provided by software: the time to develop it, the ability to maintain and enhance it, the limits on how complex a given program can be in order to be profitably sold, and the time it takes to learn and use it. This leads to the major issue facing corporate information systems today: the quality, cost, and lack of interoperability of software. While the hardware costs are plummeting, software costs are rising.

The Object Management Group (OMG) was formed to help reduce complexity, lower costs, and hasten the introduction of new software applications. OMG plans to accomplish this through the introduction of an architectural framework with supporting detailed interface specifications. These specifications will drive the industry towards interoperable, reusable, portable software components based on standard object-oriented interfaces.

OMG is an international trade association incorporated as non-profit in the United States. OMG receives funding on a yearly basis from its diverse membership of two hundred and fifty + information systems corporations. The mission of OMG is as follows:

- OMG is dedicated to maximizing the portability, reusability, and interoperability of software. OMG is the leading worldwide organization dedicated to producing the framework and specifications for commercially available object-oriented environments.
- The Object Management Group provides a Reference Architecture with terms and definitions upon which all specifications are based. OMG will create industry standards for commercially available object-oriented systems by focusing on Distributed Applications, Distributed Services and Common Facilities.
- OMG provides an open forum for industry discussion, education and promotion of OMG endorsed object technology. OMG coordinates its activities with related organizations and acts as a technology/marketing center for object-oriented software.

OMG defines the object management paradigm as the ability to encapsulate data and methods for software development. This models the "real world" through representation of program components called "objects." This representation results in faster application development, easier maintenance, reduced program complexity and reusable components. A central benefit of an object-oriented system is its ability to grow in functionality through the extension of existing components and the addition of new objects to the system.

The software concept of "objects," as incorporated into the technology of OMG, will provide solutions to the software complexities of the 1990s. Object-oriented architectures will allow applications acquired from different sources and installed on different systems to freely exchange information. Software "objects" will mirror the real world business objects they support, in the sense that the architect's blueprint mirrors a building. OMG envisions a day where users of software start up applications as they start up their cars, with no more concern about the underlying structure of the objects they manipulate than the driver has about the molecular construction of gasoline.

8.8.2.   Goals of the Object Management Group

The members of the Object Management Groups, Inc. (OMG) have a shared goal of developing and using integrated software systems. These systems should be built using a methodology that supports modular production of software; encourages reuse of code; allows useful integration across lines of developers, operating systems and hardware; and enhances long-range maintenance of that code. Members of OMG believe that the object-oriented approach to software construction best supports their goals.

Object orientation, at both the programming language and applications environment levels, provides a terrific boost in programmer productivity, and greatly lends itself to the production of integrated software systems. While not necessarily promoting faster programming, object technology allows you to construct more with less code. This is partly due to the naturalness of the approach, and also to its rigorous requirement for interface specification. What is missing is only a set of standard interfaces for interoperable software components. This is the mission of the OMG.

8.8.3. Benefits of Object Management

As mentioned above, the technological approach of object technology (or object orientation) was chosen by OMG member companies not for its own sake, but in order to attain a set of end-user goals. End users benefit in four ways from the object-oriented approach to application construction:

*   An object-oriented user interface has many advantages over more traditional user interfaces. In an object-oriented use interface, Applications Objects (computer simulated representations of real world objects) are presented to end users as objects that can be manipulated in a way that is similar to the manipulation of the real world objects. Examples of such object-oriented user interfaces are realized in systems such as Xerox Star, Apple Macintosh, NeXTSTEP from NeXT Computer, OSF Motif and HP NewWave and to a limited degree, Microsoft Windows. CAD systems are also a good example in which components of a design can be manipulated in a way similar to the manipulation of real components.

    This results in a reduced learning curve and common "look and feel" to multiple applications. It is easier to see and point than to remember and type.

*   A more indirect end-user benefit of object-oriented applications, provided that they cooperate according to some standard, is that independently developed general purpose applications can be combined in a user-specific way. It is OMG's central purpose to create a standard that realizes interoperability between independently developed applications across heterogeneous networks of computers.

    This means that multiple software programs appear as "one" to the user of information no matter where they reside.

*   Common functionality indifferent applications (such as storage and retrieval of objects, mailing of objects, printing of objects,

creation and deletion of objects, or help and computer-based training) is realized by common shared objects leading to a uniform and consistent user interface.

Sharing of information drastically reduces documentation redundancy. Consistent access across multiple applications allows for increased focus on application creation rather than application education.

- Transition to object-oriented application technology does not make existing applications obsolete. Existing applications can be embedded (with different levels of integration) in an object-oriented environment.

Pragmatic migration of existing applications gives users control over their computing resources, and how quickly their resources change.

Likewise, application developers benefit from object technology and object-oriented standards. These benefits fall into two categories:

- Through encapsulation of object data (making data accessible only in a way controlled by the software that implements the object), applications are built in a truly modular fashion, preventing unintended interference. In addition, it is possible to build applications in an incremental way, preserving correctness during the development process.
- By reusing existing components, specifically, when the OMG standard is in effect, thereby standardizing interaction between independently developed applications (and application components), cost and lead time can be saved by making use of existing implementations of object classes.

In developing standards, OMG keeps these benefits of object orientation in mind, together with a set of overall goals:

- Heterogeneity. Integration of applications and facilities must be available across heterogeneous networks of systems independent of networking transports and operating systems.

- Customization options. Common Facilities must be customizable in order to meet specific end-user or organizational requirements and preferences.
- Scope. The scope of OMG adopted technology is characterized by both work group support and mission critical applications.
- Management and control. Issues such as security, recovery, interruptability, auditing and performance are examined.
- Internationalization. As OMG is itself an international group, the standard reflects built-in support for internationalization of software.
- Technical standards. Standards to meet these user goals are the central goal of the OMG, as well as the content of [the Object Management Architecture Guide].

8.8.4. Object Management Architecture

The Object Request Broker component of the Object Management Architecture is the communications heart of the standard. This is referred to commercially as CORBA (Common Object Request Broker Architecture). It provides an infrastructure allowing objects to communicate, independent of the specific platforms and techniques used to implement the addressed objects. The Object Request Broker component will guarantee portability and interoperability of objects over a network of heterogeneous systems.

The Object Services component standardizes the life cycle management of objects. Functions are provided to create objects (the Object Factory), to control access to objects, to keep track of relocated objects and to control the relationship between species of objects (class management). The Object Services component provides the generic environment in which single objects can perform their tasks. Standardization of Object Services leads to consistency over different applications and improved productivity for the developer.

The Common Facilities component provides a set of generic applications functions that can be configured to the specific requirements of a specific configuration. Examples are printing facilities, database facilities, and electronic mail facilities. Standardization leads to uniformity in generic operations and to options for end users to configure their configurations (as opposed to configuring individual applications).

The Application Objects part of the architecture represents those application objects performing specific tasks for users. One application is typically built from a large number of basic object classes, partly specific for the application, partly from the set of Common Facilities. New classes of application objects can be built by modification of existing classes through generalization or specialization of existing classes (inheritance) as provided by Object Services. The multi-object class approach to application development leads to improved productivity for the developer and to options for end users to combine and configure their applications.

8.8.5. The OMG Object Model: Overview

This model defines a common object semantics for specifying the externally visible characteristics of objects in a standard and implementation-independent way. The common semantics characterize objects that exist in an OMG-compliant system. These systems perform operations and maintain state for objects.

The externally visible characteristics of objects are described by an interface which consists of operation signatures. The external view of both object behavior and object state (information needed to alter the outcome of a subsequent operation) are modeled in terms of operation signatures.

Objects are grouped into types and individual objects are instances of their respective types. A type determines what operations can be applied to its instances. Types participate in subtype/supertype relationships which affect the set of operations that are applicable to their instances.

Types also have implementations. An implementation of an object type is typically a set of data structures that constitute a stored representation, and a set of methods or procedures that provide the code to implement each of the operations whose signature is defined by the type.

Implementation details are encapsulated by operations, and never directly exposed in the external interface. For example, the stored representation is only observable or changeable through an operation request. The OMG Object Model formally says nothing about implementations of a type other than that they exist and that there can be multiple implementations for a given type (although it is not a requirement that systems support multiple implementations).

The OMG Object Model defines a core set of requirements that must be supported in any system that complies with the Object Model standard. This set of required capabilities is called the Core Object Model and is described in section 4.2 of [the OM Architecture Guide]. The core serves as the basis for portability and interoperability of object systems across all technologies and across implementations within technology domains.

While the Core Object Model serves as the common ground, the OMG Object Model also allows for extensions to the Core to enable even greater commonality within different technology domains. The Object Model defines the concept of components which are compatible extensions to the Core Object Model but are not required to be supported by all systems. For example, relationships are defined as components. The OMG OM Components Guide contains descriptions of components that have been accepted as a standard.

The Object Model also defines a mechanism, called profiles, for technology domains to group pertinent components. Profiles are groups of components that combine to serve as a useful set of extensions for particular domains. For example, a subset of components could be combined to form an Object Database profile of a PCTE profile.

An application that is "OMA-compliant" consists of a set of interworking classes and instances that interact via the ORB [as defined below]. Compliance therefore means conformance to the OMA and the protocol definitions and [ORB] enables objects to make and receive requests and responses.

- Object Services (OS) is a collection of services with object interfaces that provide basic functions for realizing and maintaining objects.
- Common Facilities (CF) is a collection of classes and object interfaces that provide general purpose capabilities, useful in many applications.

- Application Objects (AO) are specific to particular end-user applications.

In general terms, the Application Objects and Common Facilities have an application orientation while the Object Request Broker and Object Services are concerned more with the "system" or infrastructure aspects of distributed object management. Common Facilities may, however, provide higher-level services, such as transactions and versioning, that make use of primitives provided within Object Services.

The three categories (Object Services, Common Facilities and Application Objects) reflect a partitioning in terms of functions, from those basic to most applications or common enough to broad classes of applications to standardize, to those too application-specific or special-purpose to standardize at this time; thus, the Object Request Broker, Object Services and Common Facilities will be the focus of OMG standardization efforts.

In general, Object Services, Common Facilities, and Application Objects all intercommunicate using the Object Request Broker. Objects may also use non-object interfaces to external services, but these are outside the scope of the OMA. Although not explicit in the Reference Model, objects may (or may not) communicate with the Object Services via object interfaces. For example, the addition of a new class may be cast as a request to an object that provides this service, but equivalently, it could be performed by editing a class definition script or a C++ include file.

The Application Objects and Common Facilities use and provide functions and services via object interfaces. In general, objects can issue as well as process requests. Thus, objects categorized as Application Objects can provide services for other applications or facilities. For example, an applications specific service, such as printer rendering, could be cast as an Application Object that is invoked by a common facility, such as a print queue. Equally, objects categorized as common facilities may use services provided elsewhere.

It is important to note that applications need only provide or use OMA-compliant interfaces to participate in the Object Management Architecture. They need not themselves be constructed using the object-oriented paradigm. This also applies to the provision of Object Services. For example, existing relational or object-oriented database management systems could be used to provide some or all of the Object Services. Figure 8.6 shows how existing applications, external tools and system support software can be embedded as objects that participate in the Object Management Architecture, using class interface front-ends (otherwise called "adapters" or "wrappers").

The Reference Model does not impose any restrictions on how applications and Common Facilities are structured and implemented. Objects of a given application class may deal with the presentation of information, interaction with the user, "semantics," functionality, the persistent storage of data, or a combination of the above.

The OMA assumes that underlying services provided by a platform's operating system and lower-level basic services, such as network computing facilities, are available and usable by OMA implementations. Specifically, the Object Management Architecture does not address user interface support. The inter-

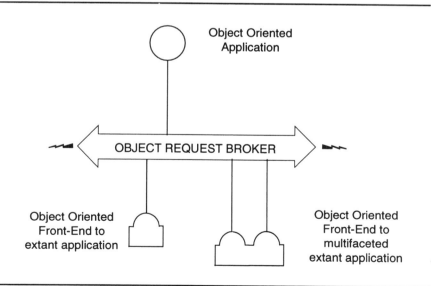

Figure 8.6.   Wrapping existing applications.

faces between applications and windowing systems or other display support are the subjects of standardization efforts outside the OMG. Eventually, however, Common Facilities may provide standard user interface classes. In addition, the Reference Model does not deal explicitly with the choice of possible binding mechanisms (e.g., compile time, load time, and run time).

8.8.6. Object Request Broker (ORB)

The Object Request Broker (ORB) provides the mechanisms by which objects transparently make and receive requests and responses. In so doing, the ORB provides interoperability between applications on different machines in heterogeneous distributed environments and seamlessly interconnects multiple object systems.

The OMG Object Model defines an object request and its associated result (response) as the fundamental interaction mechanism. A request names an operation and includes zero or more parameter values, any of which may be object names identifying specific objects. The ORB arranges for the request to be processed. This entails identifying and causing some method to be invoked that performs the operation using the parameters. After the operation terminates, the ORB conveys the results to the requester.

The ORB itself might not maintain all of the information needed to carry out its functions. In the process of conveying a request, the ORB may generate requests of its own to Object Services, or otherwise use them. For example, in order to find the specific method to be executed for a given request, the ORB might use a class dictionary service or might search run-time method libraries.

In order to satisfy the OMG Technical Objectives, the ORB is expected to address all of the following areas, at least to some degree.

• Name Services. Object name mapping services map object names in the naming domain of the requester into equivalent names in the domain of the method to be executed, and vice versa. The OMG Object Model does not require object names to be unique or universal. Object location services use the object names in the request to locate the method to perform the requested operation. Object location services may involve simple attribute lookups on objects. In practice, different object systems or domains will have locally preferred object naming schemes.

- Request Dispatch. This function determines which method to invoke. The OMG Object Model does not require a request to be delivered to any particular object. As far as the requester is concerned, it does not matter whether the request first goes to a method that then operates on the state variables of object passes as parameters, or whether it goes to any particular object in the parameter list.

- Parameter Encoding. These facilities convey the local representation of parameter values in the requester's environment to equivalent representations in the recipient's environment. To accomplish this, parameter encodings may employ standards or de facto standards (e.g., OSF/DCE, ONC/NFS/XDR, NCA/SCS/NDR, ASN.1).

- Delivery. Requests and results must be delivered to the proper location as characterized by a particular node, address, space, thread or entry point. These facilities may use standard transport protocol (e.g., TCP/UDP/IP, ISO/TPN).

- Synchronization. Synchronization primarily deals with handling the parallelism of the objects making and processing a request and the rendezvousing of the requester with the response to the request. Possible synchronization models include: asynchronous (request with no response), synchronous (request; await reply), and deferred synchronous (proceed after sending request; claim reply later).

- Activation. Activation is the housekeeping processing necessary before a method can be invoked. Activation and deactivation ("passivation") of persistent objects is needed to obtain the object state for use when the object is accessed, and save the state when it no longer needs to be accessed. For objects that hold persistent information in non-object storage facilities (e.g., files and databases), explicit requests can be made to objects to activate and deactivate themselves.

- Exception Handling. Various failures in the process of object location and attempted request delivery must be reported to requester and/or recipient in ways that distinguish them from other errors. Actions are needed to recover session resources and resynchronize requester and recipient. The ORB coordinates recovery housekeeping activities.

- Security Mechanisms. The ORB provides security enforcement mechanisms that support higher-level security control and policies. These mechanisms ensure the secure conveyance of requests among objects. Authentication mechanisms ensure the identities of requesting and receiving objects, threads, address spaces, nodes, and communication routes. Protection mechanisms assure the integrity of data being conveyed and assure that the data being communicated and the fact of communication are accessible only to authorized parties. Access enforcement mechanisms enforce access and licensing policies.

9

The Future and Evolution of Database Management

There are many new terms that are being used to describe the database systems of the future. Knowledgebases, intelligent databases, neural databases, and database machines are but a few of the many terms that are being used to describe the future of this technology.

9.1. HYPERMEDIA

Hypermedia has become a very popular term within the arena of database systems. Many PC-based systems and products advertise themselves as "hypermedia," but a comparison of these products shows that they have very little in common.

In basic terms, hypermedia refers to the ability of the database to incorporate audio and video information. From a database perspective, these audio and video components are simply other "sources," or media. Many databases already allow for the inclusion of graphical images, and even mainframe databases such as DB2 allow for a binary large object (BLOB) data type.

The latest craze within PC-based systems is the inclusion of "WAV" files. These files consist of binary audio information and always have the .WAV suffix, such as HORN.WAV. These files create predetermined sound effects and can be triggered by events within the system. For example, Microsoft Windows uses video-clip files, which allow for the inclusion of moving videos within the database.

Many very flashy database systems have been created by the addition of audio and video, and Microsoft has introduced the term OLE (pronounced oh-lay), which refers to their Object Linking and Embedding techniques.

From a database perspective, these new forms of information are not a problem for the database designer. Sound effects and moving images are stored in the database just like conventional information, and are retrieved on request just as traditional information is retrieved. The problem with hypermedia lies in the effective design and presentation of the hypermedia information.

Microsoft's product for object linking and embedding (OLE) allows divergent media to be incorporated into a single application. OLE runs under the Microsoft Windows product and allows a user to bundle audio, video, and graphics from any source in the Windows domain.

The term "hyper" in a hypermedia system refers to the ability of the system to allow links, or calls, to other components within the system that contain ancillary information. These hypertext links are commonly used within Windows environments and allow the user of the system to dynamically move to another area of interest. This concept is analogous to the "also see" references within an encyclopedia. Some text-based databases, such as the Folio® database, allow for linking between textual items.

The real problem with the development of hypermedia systems is the presentation style of the system. Many vendors create hypermedia shells that allow a database designer to add hypertext links to the applications, and it is very simple for a novice to create a system that takes advantage of sound and video. Unfortunately, many of these systems suffer from an artistic overload. Data processing professionals often have trouble with the "feel" for the dynamics of a effective presentation system, and the delivered products are often "noisy" and distracting.

Today, the development of hypermedia systems is done with the use of professional choreographers, who use many design techniques more familiar to advertising professionals than to computer programmers. Hypermedia systems are "storyboarded," and the logical flow of the presentation is mapped out with an emphasis on the aesthetic quality of the system. This has major implications for the future of database systems design. The tools for the linear presentation of textual material are now so sophisticated that an end user can develop a hypermedia system. More important than technical skill will be a feel for artistic design and presentation graphics.

9.2.   A RETURN TO CENTRALIZED DATA

As corporations begin to realize that the widespread distribution of their data resources has caused severe problems, there will be a movement to the "data warehouse" concept.

9.3.   THE RETURN OF CLIENT-SERVER

From a data management viewpoint, the very same problems that led to the invention of the first commercial databases are now returning. Thirty years ago the industry was in the age of

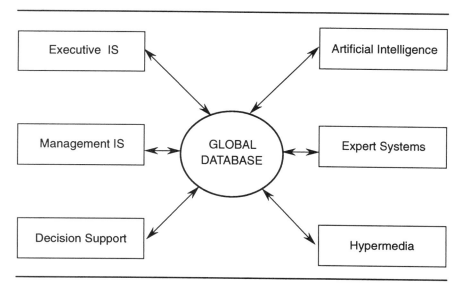

Figure 9.1.   The return of the global data repository.

"departmental computing" whereby each small area within an organization had its own data processing staff, its own systems, and worst of all, its own data and data structures. This lack of data sharing is now returning as more departments are abandoning the mainframe and developing their own systems on PC platforms or midrange computers.

One must remember that the impetus behind downsizing is primarily monetary. There is no reason to migrate from a mainframe to smaller systems except for the cheaper MIPS that are available on the smaller machines. Unfortunately, many companies are not only distributing their processing, they are distributing their data, often with disastrous results.

As more and more companies learn that distributing their data can cause problems for the corporation, we will see a move toward recentralization of data. This doesn't mean a return to the mainframe as we know it, but it does mean that very large amounts of data will be managed and distributed to all platforms within the company.

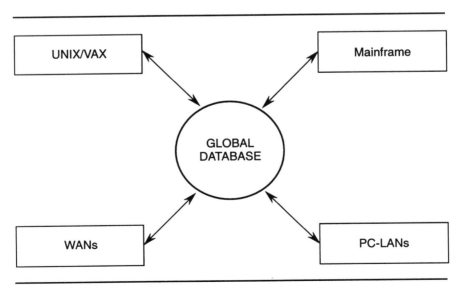

Figure 9.2.   Distributed processing: centralized data.

9.4.   EXPERIENTIAL DATABASES

As the cost of computer hardware continues to fall, data processing will undergo another revolution. Just as the first supercomputers went unnoticed by mainstream computer professionals, the new hardware technology will emerge with a whisper. However, the implications for the way people think about databases will be dramatic.

Peripheral sensors have been developed that are far superior to human peripheral senses. We have cameras that can supposedly read a newspaper headline from outer space and "ears" that can hear far better than our own, but we have never recreated the cognitive ability of even the most primitive animal. Every second, the human mind processes thousands of bits (or more) of information. We perceive the distant humming of fluorescent light bulbs, the pressure of our bodies against our chairs, and many other perceptions that are unknown to our conscious mind. Numerous researchers in human cognition hypothesize that the human mind never forgets; what is lost when a memory is "forgotten" is the ability to recall the data, and not the data itself. Oliver Sacks, the famous brain surgeon portrayed in the movie "Awakenings," related a story in his fascinating book *The Man Who Mistook His Wife for a Hat*. Doctor Sacks was performing brain surgery on a conscious patient when stimulation to a specific area of the brain caused the patient to remember a long-forgotten incident. "Remembering" is not really an appropriate term, because the patient "relived" the incident and described a scene from her childhood in such detail that she could sing along with a tune playing on the Victrola.

When computers advance to the point where storage capacity approaches the capacity of the human mind, there will be a movement toward "experiential" database machines that perceive the world around them and process information in a fashion similar to that of the human mind.

Is Human Cognition Rational?

Computers have long been able to learn from experience. Early database experiments in the 1960s demonstrated that a naive computer could learn the rules to simple games by playing the game with another computer that knew the game. However, human reasoning often differs from computer reasoning, often in very fundamental ways. An excellent example happened during World War II, when the Allied forces were planning bombing raids on Germany. Attempts at bombing targets in Germany had proved disastrous, with well over one-half of the aircraft lost, and a primitive computer was engaged to solve the problem of delivering the maximum bomb load while minimizing the amount of lives lost.

The computer was able to prove that less lives would be lost if a smaller number of planes were sent on the missions. Each of these planes would carry double the bomb load, and just enough fuel to reach their target. After dropping their bombs, the crew would bail out and take their chances within German territory.

Assume, for the point of this argument, that the statistical conclusion was correct, and that less lives would be lost if these one-way trips were adopted.

The members in the Eighth Air Force were somewhat less than elated with this proposed solution and elected to ignore the study. The idea of drawing straws for one-way trips to Germany was abhorrent to the crew members, even though they had a much higher probability of survival. Ultimately the air crews decided to ignore the study, and hundreds of American lives were lost as a direct result of "irrational" human cognition.

"Experiential" databases are those that will perceive from experience. These databases will be able to process information at a rate of 10,000 transactions per second, and will be able to store many hundreds of terabytes of data.

Such a system would need to be able to perceive and act upon stimuli in the world. In order to do so, a model would need to be developed that would allow the database to retain information in a fashion similar to that of the human mind. Sigmund Freud postulated that human memory was persistent. All memories

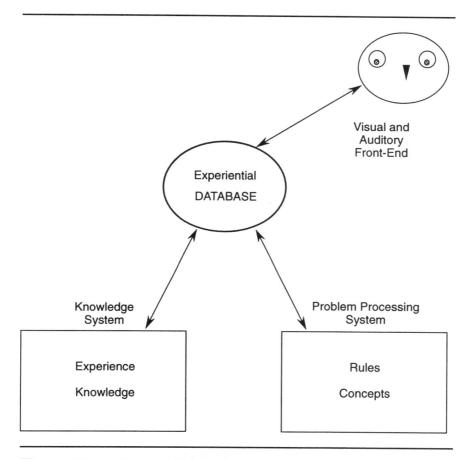

Figure 9.3.   Experiential databases.

were retained within the brain, but most were inaccessible. These inaccessible, or "unconscious," memories and experiences were nonetheless present, and served to guide the decision-making abilities of the human organism. Other psychologists have postulated that the human mind has very little ability to address detailed memory, and the human mind "filters" out the unneeded stimuli, storing only that which is required for the organism. This filtering mechanism is activated by the priorities that are set by the conscious mind. For example, a pessimist chooses to ignore positive stimuli, instead focusing on the bad events of the day. Emotional reaction also governs what is stored in the mind. The human mind "represses," or blocks, events that are unacceptable to the conscious mind and would therefore interrupt the functioning of the organism. These types of filtering devices will need to be incorporated into the database memory processors, and a great deal will be learned about the relationship between human and computer cognition.

9.5.   VOICE RECOGNITION DATABASE ACCESS

Recognizing a human voice is one of the very first things a human organism learns after birth, and a method would need to be devised that would allow voice access to the database manager. Unfortunately, computers have had dismal results when learning to parse and understand human English. It is relatively simple to digitize the sound waves for processing by the computer, but it is very difficult to get a computer to partition the sounds into words and to recognize where the words begin and end. For example, it is very difficult to teach a computer to recognize that "bus station" is two words, because the sounds run together when they are spoken.

Another problem is voice recognition of context-sensitive grammar. Even a child understands what it means when someone says, "Mary had a little lamb," but a present-day computer will be unable to resolve the verb "had." What do you mean, Mary "had" a little lamb? Did she buy the lamb, did she eat the lamb, exactly how did she "have" this lamb?

However, to simply determine the context of some spoken English has been a difficult but not insurmountable task. Technology *has* progressed to the point where computers can isolate individual spoken words, and can also spell the words according to their context. "Please WRITE to Mr. WRIGHT, RIGHT now" is an example of context-sensitive spelling.

After the spoken words and their individual meanings have been determined, the next step is to derive the meaning from the sentence. Nonstructured access to databases has long been of interest to researchers, and several products have come to the marketplace. Computer Associates® markets a product called Online

English®, which claims to allow nonstructured query against their IDMS database product. Other vendors have created tools that allow macros for the classification of database queries. For example, a user could state: "All salespeople who have not sold 3000 units this month are turkeys." This establishes a "condition set" for the word turkey, and a subsequent query—"Show me the turkeys"—will produce a list of salespeople who have sold less than 3000 units.

Some of this research deals with the translation of English into foreign languages. A tool was built that would translate English into Russian, and a reverse component was designed to translate Russian into English. The individual components worked relatively well when presented with well-structured sentences, but more obtuse English produced humorous results. For example, the phrase "The spirit is willing but the flesh is weak" was translated into Russian, and then back into English. When the translation was complete, the phrase said, "The vodka is good, but the meat is rotten."

Savvy®, a database query product by Excalibur Corporation, performs in the same fashion. For example, an employee database could be queried with the statement "How long has Joe been with us?" Savvy will respond by stating, "Are you asking for Joe's date of birth, or Joe's date of hire?"

West Publishing Company has recently released a tool called Natural®, which provides nonstructured query against its vast legal database. West claims that the researcher only needs to state a general concept, and Natural will create a structured query on behalf of the user, returning the desired information.

Query By Example (QBE®) is a database retrieval tool by IBM that allows users to query their tables without learning SQL. Users of the DB2 database are presented with a list of database fields that they can combine to create "sample" tables containing all the columns and rows that they desire. The user could also specify selection constraints. QBE will generate the appropriate SQL for the users and return their query in tabular format.

Despite the relatively primitive state of today's technology, the next thirty years will see a revolution in ad hoc database access. Tools will be devised that allow a user to state a query to an intelligent front-end, which will parse the meaning from the statement and return the results.

10

Object-Oriented Databases and Advanced Systems

There has been a great deal of interest in the application of object-oriented databases to advanced systems, such as expert systems and decision support systems. These systems have been used to solve semi-structured and even unstructured problems. Traditionally, these types of systems combine "inference engines" and relational databases in order to store the knowledge-processing components. Unfortunately, very little work has been done with the application of object-oriented databases to these types of systems. In fact, the birth of object-oriented techniques corresponds with the use of the SIMULA® language, which is used as a modeling component of decision support systems.

10.1. EXPERT SYSTEMS

Expert system is a term used very loosely in the computer community. The term "expert systems" has been used to describe anything from a spreadsheet program to any program containing an IF statement.

In general terms, an expert system is a system that models the well-structured decision process of an individual and applies that reasoning process to a real-world situation. Any decision that has quantifiable rules can have the rules stored in an *infer-*

ence engine. An inference engine is used to drive the information-gathering component of the system, and to eventually arrive at the solution to the problem.

It has been said that an expert system makes a decision "for" the user, while a decision support system makes a decision "with" the user. This is essentially true, because an expert system makes no provision for human intuition in the decision-making process. Many real-world management decisions do not require human intuition. For example, one of the crucial jobs of a retail manager is the decision of what goods to order, how many goods to order, and when to order the goods. This decision can be represented by a model called economic order quantity (EOQ). If the EOQ equation knows the velocity at which the goods are leaving the retail store, the reorder time for the goods, the average time on the shelf, and the cost of the goods, the computer can confidently produce automatic daily reports on which goods to order and how many to order.

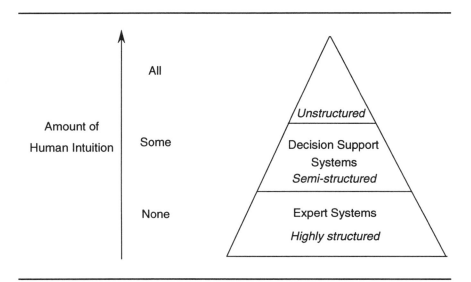

Figure 10.1.   Problem structure and human intuition.

10.2. DECISION SUPPORT TECHNOLOGY

A decision support system (DSS) is generally defined as the type of system that deals with the semi-structured problem, that is, there is a structured component to the task as well as a component that involves human intuition. The well-structured components are the decision-rules, which are stored as the problem-processing system, while the intuitive, or creative, component is left to the user.

Examples of Semi-Structured Problems

Choosing a spouse
Building a factory
Choosing magazine artwork
Building a new sports car
Designing a Graphical User Interface (GUI) for an OODBMS

Decision support technology recognizes that there are many tasks that requiring human intuition. For example, the process of choosing a stock portfolio is a task having both structured and intuitive components. Certainly, there are rules associated with choosing a stock portfolio, such as diversification of the stocks and choosing an acceptable level of risk. These factors can be easily quantified and stored in a database system. This allows the user of the system to do "what if" scenarios. However, because a system has well-structured components, does this mean that the entire decision process is well-structured?

One of the best ways to tell if a decision process is semi-structured is to ask yourself if people with the same level of knowledge demonstrate different levels of skill. For example, there are many stockbrokers, all with about the same level of knowledge about the stock market; but clearly, people demonstrate different levels of skill when assembling stock portfolios.

Computer simulation is one area that is used heavily within the modeling components of decision support systems. In fact,

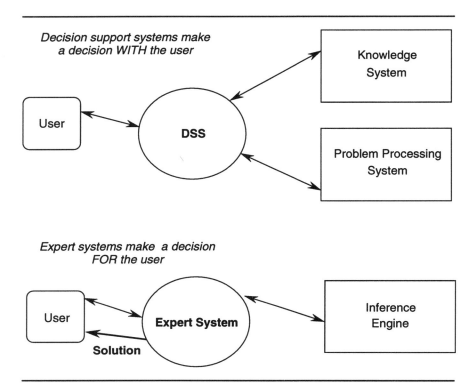

Figure 10.2. Decision support systems vs. expert systems.

one of the first object-oriented languages was SIMULA. SIMULA was used as a driver for these "what if" scenarios and was incorporated into decision support systems in order to allow the user to model a particular situation. The user would create a scenario with objects, and these objects were subjected to a set of predefined behaviors.

The general characteristics of a decision support system include:

1. **A nonrecurring problem is to be solved.** DSS technology is used primarily for novel and unique modeling situations where the use is required to simulate the behavior of some real-world problem.

2. **DSS requires human intuition.** This means that the DSS makes the decision *with* the user, unlike expert systems, which make the decision *for* the user.
3. **DSS requires knowledge of the problem being solved.** Unlike an expert system, where the user provides answers to well-structured questions, decision support systems require the user to thoroughly understand the problem being solved. For example, a financial decision support system, such as DSSF would require the user to understand the concept of a stock "beta." Beta is the term used to measure the covariance of an individual stock against the behavior of the market as a whole. Without an understanding of the concepts, a user would be unable to effectively utilize a decision support system.
4. **DSS may produce more than one acceptable answer.** Unlike an expert system, which usually produces a single, finite answer to a problem, a decision support system deals with problems that have a domain, or a range, of acceptable solutions. For example, a user of DSSF may find that there are many "acceptable" stock portfolios that match the selection criteria of the user. Another good example is a manager who needs to place production machines onto an empty warehouse floor. The goal would be to maximize the throughput of work in process from raw materials to finished goods. Clearly, there would be more than one acceptable way of placing the machines onto the warehouse floor in order to achieve this goal. This is called the "state space" approach to problem solving where a solution domain is specified and the user works to create models to achieve the desired goal state.

Decision support systems also allow the user to create "what if" scenarios. These are essentially modeling tools that allow the user to define an environment and then simulate the behavior of that environment under changing conditions.

For example, the user of DSSF would create a hypothetical stock portfolio and then direct the DSS to model the behavior of that stock portfolio under different market conditions. Once these behaviors are specified, the user may vary the contents of the portfolio and view the results.

There has been a great debate about the role of intuition in this type of problem solving. Decision support systems allow the user to control the decision-making process, applying their own decision-making rules and intuition to the process. However, there is a great deal of debate as to whether artificial intelligence can be used to manage the intuitive component of these systems.

For example, most of us enjoyed playing tic-tac-toe when we were children, and we probably spent many hours playing this game. Why is it that now, as adults, we do not return home from a long day at the office and play tic-tac-toe? The answer is that we have now come to perceive that tic-tac-toe is a well-structured task and that once one knows the rules it is impossible to win the game when playing against someone else who knows the rules. This perception of tic-tac-toe as being a semi-structured game may apply to other situations in problem solving.

An excellent example of this principle happened when a large soup manufacturer hired a team of knowledge engineers to capture the expertise of an employee who was about to retire. This employee had been with the company more than thirty years, and he seemed to intuitively know exactly what to do to correct the ongoing problems. The managers at the company fully expected the knowledge engineers to create a decision support system. That is, they expected that the employee used human intuition to solve the problem and their only hope was that the knowledge engineers could capture the structured components of his problem-solving abilities.

As the knowledge engineers proceeded with their work, it became evident that the individual was applying a very complex set of well-structured rules to the problems. At first, the individual was presented with a problem to which he would reply " I have a feeling" and then accurately describe the solution. When pressed, the individual remembered a similar situation that had happened decades ago for which the solution was the same. What had first seemed to be intuition was in reality the solution to a long-forgotten problem, which manifested itself as a hunch. These hunches, or intuitive guesses, were in reality the application of the solution to a well-structured problem that the individual could not remember until he was pressed for details.

The principle is quite simple. What is at first perceived as intuition may not be intuition at all, but rather the application of decision rules to a very complex problem. As it turned out, the knowledge engineers were able to completely quantify the decision-making processes of the individual and were able to deliver an expert system rather than a decision support system. The employee was able to retire, knowing that all of his problem-solving abilities had been captured and implemented using an expert system with an inference engine.

There are many circumstances in the real world in which a problem is classified as intuitive or creative when in reality the problem is well-structured, but characterized by hundreds or even thousands of complex decision rules that interact together in a factorial number of conditions. These types of complex problems may generate millions of decision paths that need to be traversed in order to be solved.

This tendency to characterize complex, well-structured problems as being unsolvable is evident in many real-world situations. For example, there are those who claim that computer technology will never advance to the point where it can be used to predict natural disasters such as hurricanes and tornadoes. They argue that small events such as the flapping of a butterfly's wings in the Amazon basin can set off a chain of events that can affect weather patterns in North America. They argue that weather events are chaotic and therefore unstructured.

This is analogous to the child who argues that tic-tac-toe is a semi-structured game that requires skill and intuition. Just because a problem is very large and has trillions of variables such as predicting tornadoes or earthquakes is not a justification for labeling the problem as unsolvable.

Consider the nature of creativity. How could one program a computer to appreciate art? Could a computer program be devised that could "appreciate" the bold, colorful strokes of a Van Gogh, or the detail and facial expressions of a Rembrandt portrait?

Also consider individuals who are famous for their intuition. Could a computer program be written that could replicate Lee Iacocca's instincts when it comes to managing large corporations? Such individuals will be glad to say that their eight-figure incomes are justified because of their unique abilities at solving intangible problems.

There are two sides of this argument. There are those who

argue that there are situations in the real world that are naturally chaotic and can therefore never be accurately modeled with computer techniques. Conversely, there are those who argue that creativity and intuition do not imply that a problem is without structure, and that techniques will be devised that allow computers to come up with "novel" ideas and approaches to problems that are unsolvable with today's technology.

The problem lies with describing creative thought, and applying rules even where the rules do not have any concrete existence. Albert Einstein, the creator of the theory of relativity, was once asked how he made the profound mental leap that allowed him to forever change the paradigm of natural law. Einstein at first replied that it "just came to him" and he was unable to give any concrete explanation for his intuitive brilliance. However, upon further questioning, he remembered that he developed a mental model that he used to develop his theory. Einstein pictured an elevator falling at the speed of light and wondered: "If a hole were cut in this elevator, would light enter the hole?" Using this model, he developed a conceptual framework for the problem to be solved.

For the past three decades, computer researchers have attempted to program skill and intuition into computer systems. The earliest research was done with non-zero-sum games such as chess and checkers. Researchers were able to prove in the 1960s that computers could be devised that could learn and transfer knowledge by interacting with other computers. An experiment was devised in which two computers played tic-tac-toe. One computer was programmed with the set of rules for tic-tac-toe and the other computer was programmed to learn from experience. At first, the naive computer lost every game, but as the number of trials increased, the naive machine slowly began to infer the rules of the game. Eventually the naive machine played tic-tac-toe as well as the experienced machine, demonstrating the principle that computers could be taught to learn experientially.

But what about games that undeniably require skill? Studies were done using the game of chess to determine if a computer could be programmed to apply the same intuitive knowledge as a chess Grand Master. The earliest attempts used a method whereby a probability tree was created, one for each possible

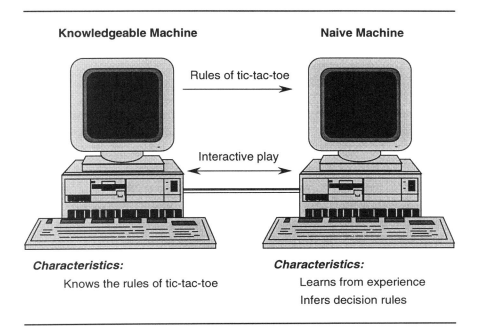

Knowledgeable Machine

Rules of tic-tac-toe

Interactive play

Naive Machine

Characteristics:

Knows the rules of tic-tac-toe

Characteristics:

Learns from experience

Infers decision rules

Figure 10.3. Experiential learning.

movement of the chess pieces. This tree was then extrapolated for numerous moves down the game, and this simulation produced a very large probability tree. The computer then chose the path that offered the highest probability of success. In actual trials, these programs played chess relatively well, but were almost always defeated by expert chess players. The researchers then decided to question human experts on chess and develop a model that more closely approximated their cognitive processes. Unlike the computer, human chess experts narrowed down their probability analysis to a small set of moves, and carried these moves forward for many more iterations than the computer model. When these human "heuristics" were programmed into the computer, the chess-playing behavior improved, and some computers have won the title of chess Grand Master.

Simulation modeling is a critical component of most decision support systems. The user of the simulation is required to define an environment that includes objects, attributes of objects, and the behavior of the objects. Non-object-oriented simulation languages such as Simscript and GPSS allow the simulator to develop a framework that is remarkably similar to the framework of object-oriented databases.

Clearly, object-oriented techniques could be very beneficial for this type of modeling. If a user could have the ability to encapsulate objects and make the objects "behave" in their simulation, the overall model could be constructed with meaningful icons rather than mathematical constructs. For example, a modeler who wanted to simulate the behavior of people waiting for service could define a "person" object with all of the behaviors required for the model.

11

Internals of Object-Oriented Databases

11.1. CONCURRENT PROCESSING

In order for an object-oriented database to manage simultaneous updates by many users, a method must be devised to ensure that each object is updated without interference by other concurrent users. Relational databases use the concept of record locking. As a row of data is retrieved from a table, the row ID is locked, such that the record is unavailable for update by any other transactions until the unit of work has been completed. These locking mechanisms are only useful for managing update and insert operations.

Consider the situation where one user is viewing the record for customer 123 while another user is simultaneously viewing this record. User number 1 updates the customer information. User number 2 is unaware that this change has taken place because his unit of work has already ended and the record appeared on his online screen before user 1 made the change. This pseudo-conversational mode requires the database manager to issue locks upon the retrieval of any database record because any user could issue an update at any time, resulting in "update anomalies" whereby information is overlaid.

Under the above scenario, if user 2 would then update the information for customer 123, the changes made by user 1 would be overlaid with user 2's information. The problem with indiscriminate record locking in pseudo-conversational mode is that once a record is displayed on the screen, the record lock must be maintained for the duration of that user's session. For example, a user could call up the information for customer 123 at which time an update lock would be placed on this customer record, prohibiting anyone else from retrieving with intent to update. User 1 could then hold this lock for minutes or even hours before releas-

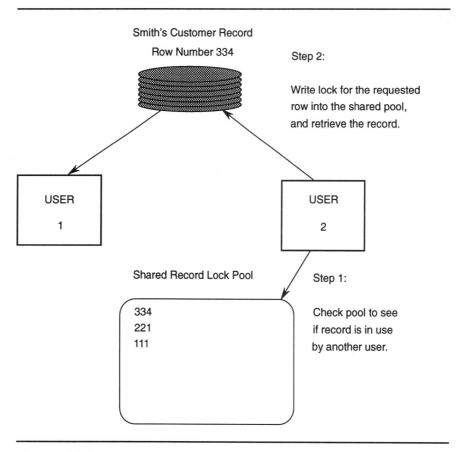

Figure 11.1. Database concurrency control.

ing this record back to the database. Unfortunately, the only way to alleviate this problem is to run the online sessions in a fully conversational mode. A fully conversational task is one in which the task-termination checkpoint is not written to the database until the actual record is released.

For object-oriented databases, a customer screen may consist of objects from different areas of the database. Because there is no one-to-one correspondence between an object and its data components, a record-locking mechanism for a single object might need to lock numerous rows from numerous tables in the database.

For most commercial database systems, record locks are held in RAM memory and consist of the row ID for relational databases, or the DB-KEY for CODASYL records. A DB-KEY is used by some databases to uniquely identify a record, and consists of a database page (physical block), and an offset, or displacement, into the database page.

Before any database retrieval occurs, the storage pool is scanned to be sure that no other active programs have requested the record with intent to update. If the program has set a lock on the desired record, the database will return a message code that can be trapped by the application. The application can then decide to wait for the record or to abort the transaction and provide the appropriate message to the user. Because most transactions are relatively short, this type of contention seldom occurs. However, background tasks or large updates can often create thousands of record locks. In traditional database systems, this problem is overcome by issuing commit statements, which release all pending locks that were issued since the beginning of the job, or since a previous commit checkpoint.

11.2. TRANSACTION LOGGING MECHANISMS

In order to maintain data integrity within an object-oriented database, a scheme must be devised that will allow the system to recover from hardware or software failure. Software failure occurs when a unit of work abnormally terminates (abends) prior to its normal end of processing. Under this circumstance, the program is rolled back and the database is returned to the state it existed in prior to the start of the task.

Hardware failure can occur when disk media becomes unusable. When this happens, the object-oriented database must allow for the recovery of the bad media and a roll-forward of all objects up to the time at which the disk failure occurred. Hardware failure could also occur if the system were to crash in the middle of online processing. When the database is restarted, a warm-start utility must be invoked to detect all unfinished transactions and to roll them back to their state at the beginning of the task.

This roll-forward and roll-back capability is accomplished by taking "before" and "after" images of all objects. In order to ensure that data integrity is maintained, these before and after images are written to a log file prior to physically updating the object in the database. In the case where a software problem occurs, a user-exit will detect the abnormal termination of the task and will go to the system logs to apply all of the before images, restoring all of the objects to their initial state. In the case of media failure, the Database Administrator will restore the database using the most current backup copies, and then apply the after images from the database log to this newly restored database, rolling it forward to the time of the disk crash.

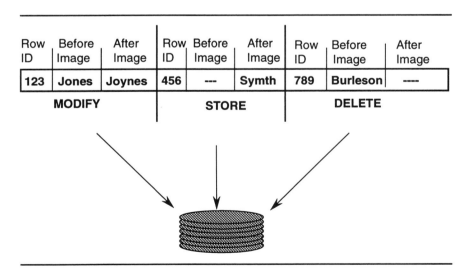

Row ID	Before Image	After Image	Row ID	Before Image	After Image	Row ID	Before Image	After Image
123	Jones	Joynes	456	---	Symth	789	Burleson	----
MODIFY			STORE			DELETE		

Figure 11.2. Database logging mechanism.

Database logs contain four types of records. A begin-job checkpoint is issued at the start of each program within the system. This record contains a unique system identifier for the program and the precise time that the task was invoked. Following the begin-job checkpoint, a series of "before" and "after" images are written to the log. These before and after images contain the run unit ID number, the object ID number (OID), and the complete contents of the data that has changed. In the case of an object deletion, only the before image is written to the log. Conversely, in the case of an add operation, only the after image is written to the log. A run unit may terminate in one of two ways. If the program successfully completes, an *end job* checkpoint is written to the log containing the run unit ID and the precise time of task termination.

For high-volume update transactions, the program may issue *commit* checkpoints. A commit checkpoint consists of the run unit ID and the time at which the checkpoint was issued. Commit checkpoints serve two functions within the object-oriented database. First, a commit checkpoint will release any record locks that are being held within the database storage pool. The commit checkpoint also serves as the termination point for any roll-back activity. For example, the database will detect an abnormally terminated task, will go to the logs, and will apply all *before* object images until either a *commit* checkpoint or a *begin* checkpoint is encountered.

In the event of a system crash, the database startup routine must be directed to interrogate the system logs to see if there are any abnormally terminated tasks from the last database session. If the Database Administrator detects an abnormal condition, he or she will go to the logs and apply the before images for all of these tasks, thereby ensuring that each object in the database maintains its integrity.

As object-oriented databases enter mainstream business systems, a method will need to be devised to allow these object-oriented databases to remain running for indefinite periods of time. These 24-hours-a-day, seven-days-a-week systems present a difficult problem for the maintenance of backup tapes. In a normal environment, the database is shut down and a full-image copy of the files are taken before the database is restarted. However, a 24 × 7 database cannot be stopped while backups are taken. In other

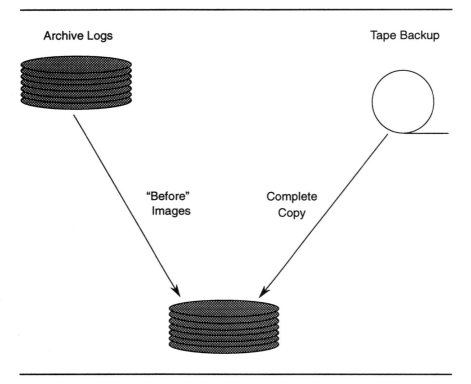

Figure 11.3.   Database recovery: rolling forward.

words, the database may be updated DURING the backup session. In order to restore a database from this type of backup, the backup utility must be carefully synchronized with the system logs. This method is sometimes called a flying dump. When the backup begins, the database system is quiesced. A *quiesce* is a circumstance where the database does not allow any new transactions to begin until all in-process transactions have completed. This creates one brief moment in time where the database has no active work. At this precise moment a synchronization point is written to the system logs and the backup begins. Because the backup and the system logs are in exact harmony, recovery is possible to any point in time.

Object-Oriented Database Standards

12.1.   THE ODMG OBJECT MODEL

The ODMG is a vendor organization dedicated to providing standards for object-oriented databases. The ODMG object model was developed jointly by a consortium of object-oriented database vendors, including Versant, Ontos, O2 Technology, Object Design, SunSoft, and Objectivity corporations. Notably absent was Microsoft Inc. These companies feel a sense of urgency in creating a unified standard for object-oriented databases, and they have prepared the ODMG model in the hope that all OODB vendors will adopt the model. Current commercial OODB systems are not portable across hardware platforms, and it is hoped that a joint approach toward object-oriented database architecture will create an environment whereby object-oriented systems share many characteristics, just as relational databases share common interfaces such as SQL.

Because of a lack of standards for object-oriented database architectures, most of the major OODB vendors have been creating commercial products that have very diverse internal structures. A recent effort has been made to propose a standard architecture for object-oriented database systems (Loomis et al., 1993), and this standard may become the foundation for an industrywide architecture for object-oriented databases.

The ODMG model creates an independent model that is language-independent, and object models may be bound to many different languages. ODMG develops a hierarchy of objects, with the most general object called a "denotable" object. Denotable objects may be either mutable or immutable. A mutable object may changes its values and properties, but an immutable object contains only literal values.

Within immutable objects, we find two subcategories, atomic and structured. A denotable, immutable, atomic object is represented by the same data types found in a relational database, namely CHAR, INTEGER, and FLOAT. A denotable, immutable, structured object is a literal structure such as the DATE and TIME data types.

Unlike the relational database model, the ODMG model requires that all objects are assigned an object identifier (OID) to uniquely identify the object. While it is unclear, it appears that it is not possible to reference an object by the data values in the object. For example, in a relational database one could state: SELECT * FROM ORDER WHERE ORDER_NBR = 123; this would not be possible under this object model. Rather, the ODMG model requires "database currency" to locate the object, and the system must know the OID.

The ODMG model also categorizes objects according to their lifetime within the runtime system. Temporary objects, those associated with a procedure or a process, are classified separately from "database" objects, which require external storage.

The ODMG object model also attempts to redefine the basic principles of entity/relationship modeling but carries the concept one step further, specifying directionality when navigating the data relationship.

This model also specifies navigational operators to traverse the linked-list data structures that are found in the commercial implementations of object-oriented databases. These operators are remarkably similar to the DML found in other pointer-based models such as CODASYL, and include verbs such as CREATE, ADD_MEMBER, and TRAVERSE. The model also has database operators that help maintain data integrity. These are abso-

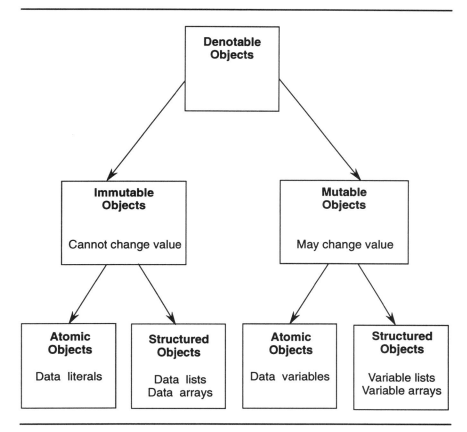

Figure 12.1.   The ODMG object model.

lutely identical to the CODASYL network data model, and have the verbs BEGIN, COMMIT, ABORT, and CHECKPOINT.

ODMG also attempts to recognize the importance of coexistence with relational databases, and the ODMG model is called a "superset" of the relational database model.

The ODMG authors state:

An important difference between the relational model and the ODMG Object Model is that the relational model does not support user-defined subtyping of the type hierarchy. Only built-in types can be used by applications. An object programmer must translate objects into the predefined structures supported by the relational DBMS in order to use the relational DBMS for persistent storage. Only the predefined, table-oriented operations supplied by SQL can be used to access the relational database. By contrast, the ODMG Object Model provides a way for application semantics to be expressed explicitly in the schema and supported directly by the OODBMS. (Loomis et al., 1993)

REFERENCE

Loomis, M., Atwood, T., Cattel, R., Duhi, J., Ferran, G., Wade, D., "The ODMG object model," *Journal of Object-Oriented Programming*, June 1993.

Appendix

Commercial Object-Oriented Databases

This appendix is a review of most of the commercial object-oriented database offerings. The text has been broken into two groups. The first group is the object-oriented databases. These are "pure" object-oriented databases, although they may support relational extensions. The second group is relational databases, which support object-oriented programming techniques.

This information has been collected from the vendors, and none of their statements has been checked for accuracy. I suspect that some of the "object-oriented" features are nothing more than GUI front-ends, but I have included all database vendors who claim to offer object-oriented technology. All products are presented in alphabetical order.

NONRELATIONAL OBJECT-ORIENTED DATABASES

Cairo—Windows NT

Microsoft Corporation, Redmond, WA

While not a true object-oriented database, Cairo is an object-oriented development environment with full database support. Cairo will use Microsoft's OLE (object linking and embedding) component to deliver a "new" data storage model. This new model will allow for extensibility, and distributed systems communication. Cairo is scheduled for release in 1994.

C-Data Manager®
Database Technologies, Brookline, MA

CDM is an object-oriented database and programming environment which allows for the creation and maintenance of class hierarchies. This tool is based on the CODASYL Network Data Model.

ENVY/Developer
Object Technology International Incorporated®, Ottawa, Canada

ENVY is a team-development environment for SmallTalk programmers. This tool enhances the standard SmallTalk environment by adding version control, configuration management, and a set of utilities. The utilities include performance analysis tools and a facility for object storage and retrieval.

Gemstone
Servio Corporation, Alameda, CA

Gemstone is a multimedia object-oriented database for midrange systems. It allows nontextual objects such as graphs, pictures, and audio to be stored and manipulated.

IDB Object Database®
Persistent Data Systems®, Pittsburgh, PA

IDB is a full-function distributed object-oriented database. IDB supports multiple inheritance and uses C as the host language.

Matisse®
Object Databases, Cambridge, MA

Matisse is an object-oriented database for client-server applications on DEC VAX and Sun workstations.

Objectivity/DB

Digital Equipment Corp.

Objectivity/DB is marketed by Digital Equipment Corporation, and the Objectivity/DB database is being used by DEC to capitalize on the trend toward object-oriented systems. Objectivity/DB is being used by DEC to develop products that will be marketed as turnkey systems. It is interesting to note that the Gain-Momentum® database product, which is used for multimedia applications, uses the Objectivity/DB as its engine. Objectivity/DB is focused primarily on the CAD/CAM marketplace. Objectivity/DB now has a tool called Objectivity/DB SQL++, which serves as an ad hoc query interface to relational databases.

ObjectStore

Object Design, Incorporated, Burlington, MA

ObjectStore is a tool that allows object persistence for C and C++ applications. ObjectStore has an online schema generation tool, and an online C debugger. ObjectStore also claims to support distributed database systems.

Ontos

ONTOS, Incorporated, Burlington, MA

Ontos is an object-oriented database for PCs using the IBM OS/2 operating system and for midrange computers. Ontos claims to support client-server and distributed database. Ontos has a graphical database administrator utility and, while not fully relational, allows SQL commands.

OpenODB

Hewlett-Packard, Palo Alto, CA

OpenODB is a full-function object-oriented database for midrange computers. OpenODB claims to support multimedia applications and object-oriented extensions that allow users to continue to use existing applications.

O2®

O2 Technology, Cambridge, MA

O2 is a full-function object-oriented database development environment. O2 includes graphical user interface (GUI) development tools, and a complete systems development environment.

Poet®

Poet Software, Santa Clara, CA

Poet allows for object persistence for C and C++ systems on midrange computers, and is also available for Windows on PC platforms. Poet claims to be able to store complex objects, and operates with Aldus.

Reflex®

Borland International, Scotts Valley, CA

Reflex is a flat-file manager for PC systems that is used to store graphics and visual information. Reflex also includes a data analysis toolset.

SMARTstore®

PROCASE Corporation, San Jose, CA

SMARTstore is an object-oriented database for midrange systems that supports concurrent users, record-level locking, and warm-start capabilities.

VERSANT

Versant Object Technology, Menlo Park, CA

Of all of the object-oriented database vendors, Versant has achieved the most media exposure. IBM has recently announced that it will be designing its repository manager with an object-oriented database engine, and it has been hinted that Versant will be the chosen vehicle. Versant claims to be an all-purpose, object-oriented distributed database, and also claims to be language-independent. Versant offers graphical administration tools and an "object archival" system that allows object data to be offloaded onto tertiary storage. Versant also allows for transactions to be nested within other transactions.

RELATIONAL/OBJECT-ORIENTED DATABASES

Actor®

The Whitewater Group, Evanston, IL

Actor is a PC object-oriented database that includes database-independent SQL class libraries. Actor can be used to create Windows applications that can access relational data from numerous platforms, including DB2 and Paradox.

Business Objects®

Business Objects, Incorporated®, Menlo Park, CA

Business Objects is a PC-based front-end for existing relational databases. This tool allows the user to define and combine objects, and then use these objects to produce a relational query. The DBA can create a domain of objects and classes, which are then mapped to the relational database. The objects are attached to the database with SQL, which is hidden from the user of the system. The user is allowed to manipulate the objects without using SQL, and the objects can be exported into word processors or spreadsheets. Business Objects is currently available for Microsoft Windows, Macintosh, and MS-DOS.

DBMagic®

Advanced Microsolutions®, Menlo Park, CA

DBMagic is a PC relational database for Windows. DBMagic claims to have a nonprocedural fourth-generation language and has object-oriented utilities for user interaction.

Hybase®

Answer Software, Cupertino, CA

Hybase is an object-oriented multimedia system for Macintosh computers. Hybase supports SQL operators, and allows users to create and access tables.

nuBASE®
Tactic Software, West Palm Beach, FL

nuBase is a relational database for Macintosh computers that has object-oriented extensions.

Omnis®
Blyth Software, Foster City, CA

Omnis is an object-oriented database for Macintosh computers. Omnis claims to support client-server systems, and includes an SQL facility for access to relational databases.

OpenODB
Hewlett-Packard, Cupertino, CA

This product is marketed by Hewlett-Packard, and has the unique feature of allowing an existing relational database to co-exist with the object-oriented engine. OpenODB is popular with users in the petroleum and chemical industries, who are unwilling to abandon their relational systems but who also wish to exploit object-oriented technology. The database storage manager is object-oriented, but this product has been reported to suffer from slow performance due to the overhead of the storage manager. OpenODB allows for the definition of class hierarchies with three modeling concepts: object, type, and function.

OpenODB uses "Types," which are similar to object classes, and "functions," which define the behaviors and data attributes of the objects. OpenODB includes a graphical browser, and allows its extended object-oriented SQL to be embedded in C, C++, CO-BOL, FORTRAN, and PASCAL.

Oracle Version 8
Oracle Corporation, Redwood Shores, CA

Oracle has announced that its next version of the popular Oracle database will provide an object-oriented strap-on to its relational engine. Deemed SQL++®, this extension to SQL will allow data manipulation of objects as well as traditional manipulation of table information. Oracle has not announced a delivery date for Version 8, but when it is delivered, it will probably become immediately popular because of the large number of existing Oracle users.

Orion®
XIDAK, Incorporated, Palo Alto, CA

Not yet available for general release, Orion claims to be a tool for the transition from relational to object-oriented databases.

Paradox (Version 4)
Borland International, Incorporated, Scotts Valley, CA

Paradox is a popular PC relational database that now offers object-oriented extensions. These extensions allow the user to manipulate objects directly and not through the relational tables.

Persistence®
Persistence Software, San Mateo, CA

Persistence is a database tool that allows C++ systems to use relational technology to store objects. Persistence also includes an automatic code generator.

Raima Object Manager®
Raima Corporation, Issaquah, WA
Raima Object Manager is an extension to the Raima database that allows object-oriented persistence for C++ applications on midrange and PC Windows systems. In addition to object persistence, Raima claims to support relationships between objects. Raima also claims to support relational access to objects.

Serius Database®
Serius Corporation, Salt Lake City, UT

Serius is a tool for Macintosh® computers that is sold as a subcomponent of the Serius Object Library. Serius allows programmers to design a system as if it were a fully relational system, and to access the tables as objects.

SPCS PrimaBase®

Scandinavian PC Systems, Incorporated®, Baton Rouge, LA

SPCS is a PC relational database for Windows. It includes an object-oriented form and report editor.

UniSQL

UniSQL, Incorporated, Austin, TX

UniSQL was developed by Dr. Wong Kim, the author of several books on object-oriented topics. UniSQL is an offering that claims to unify the relational, object-oriented, and client/server concepts into a single database. UniSQL is really an object-oriented extension to a relational database engine. UniSQL has some rather strange changes to the relational concept, such as allowing multiple values for a single database field, and even allowing an entire table to be contained within a database field. However, this data nesting capability has some advantages when designing object-oriented databases, and UniSQL also supports database triggers that can be associated with individual tables. A subversion of this product, UniSQL/M, claims to use the object-oriented model while accommodating existing relational systems, including Oracle and Sybase.

VIA/DRE

Via International Inc.,Vienna, VA

VIA is a distributed relational database for PC and midrange platforms. Facilities include SQL and C++ programming support.

Bibliography

Abiteoul, S., Kanellkis, P., Waller, E., "Method schemas," *Communications of the ACM*, 1990.

Accredited Standards Committee, X3/SPARC/DBSSG/OODBTG, Final Report of the Object-Oriented Database Task Group, September 1991.

Ahad, R., Dedo, D., "OpenODB from Hewlett-Packard: a commercial object-oriented database system," *Journal of Object-Oriented Programming*, Vol. 4, Issue 9, Feb. 1992.

Ahmed, S., Wong, A., Sriram, D., Logcher, R., "A comparison of object-oriented database management systems for engineering applications," MIT Technical Report IESL-90-03, 1990.

Alagic, A., *Object-Oriented Database Programming* (New York: Springer-Verlag Publishers, 1988).

Atkinson, D., et al., "The object-oriented database systems manifesto," *Deductive and Object-Oriented Databases* (New York: Elsevier Science Publishers, 1990).

Atwood, T., Orenstein, J., "Notes toward a standard object-oriented DDL and DML," *Computer Standards & Interfaces*, Vol. 13, 1991.

Babcock, C., "Object lessons," *Computerworld*, May 3, 1993.

Banciinon, F., *Building an Object-Oriented Database System: the*

Story of O2 (San Mateo, CA: Morgan Kaufman Publishers, 1992).

Banerjee, J., "Data model issues for object-oriented applications," *ACM Transactions on Office Information Systems*, 5(1):3–26, 1987.

Bradley, J., "An object-relationship diagrammatic technique for object-oriented database definitions," *Journal of Database Administration*, Vol. 3, Issue 2, Spring 1992.

Brathwaite, K., *Object-Oriented Database Design: Concepts and Applications* (San Diego, CA: Academic Press, 1993).

Bratsberg, S.E., "FOOD: supporting explicit relations in a fully object-oriented database," Proceedings of the IFIP TC2/WG 2.6 Working Conference, 1991.

Brown, A.W., *Object-Oriented Databases and Their Applications to Software Engineering* (New York: McGraw-Hill, 1991).

Burleson, D., "SQL generators," *Database Programming & Design*, July 1993.

Burleson, D., "Performance & tuning strategies for the very large database," *Database Programming and Design*, October 1989.

Burleson, D., Kassicieh, S., "A decision support system for scheduling," Proceedings of the International Conference, Operations Research Society of America, Chicago, IL, 1983.

Burleson, D., Kassicieh, S., Lievano, R. "Design and implementation of a decision support system for academic scheduling," *Information and Management*, Volume II, Number 2, September 1986.

Cattell, R.G.G., *Object Data Management: Object-Oriented and Extended Relational Database Systems* (Reading, MA: Addison-Wesley, 1991).

Cattell, R.G.G., Rogers, T., "Combining object-oriented and relational models of data," International Workshop on Object-Oriented Database Systems, Proceedings, Wash., DC, IEEE Computer Society Press, 1986.

Chung, Y., Fischer, G., "Illustration of object-oriented databases for the structure of a bill of materials," *Computers in Industry*, Vol. 19, June 1992.

Codd, E.F., *The Relational Model for Database Management*, Version 2 (Reading, MA: Addison-Wesley, 1990).

Comaford, C., "At long last, a true query tool for end users," *PC Week*, March 1993.

Date, C.J., *An Introduction to Database Systems* (Reading, MA; Addison-Wesley, 1990).

De Troyer, O., Keustermans, J., Meersman, R., "How helpful is object-oriented language for an object-oriented database model?," International Workshop on Object-Oriented Database Systems, Proceedings, Wash., DC, IEEE Computer Society Press, 1986.

Dittrich, K., "Object-oriented database systems: the notions and the issues," International Workshop on Object-Oriented Database Systems, Proceedings, Wash., DC, IEEE Computer Society Press, 1986.

Dittrich, K., Dayal, U., Buchmann, P., *On Object-Oriented Database Systems* (New York: Springer Verlag Publishers, 1991).

Gane, C., Sarson, T., Structured Systems Analysis: tools & techniques, St. Louis, Improved Systems Technology.

Gorman, K., Choobineh, J., "An overview of the object-oriented entity relationship model (OOERM)," Proceedings of the Twenty-Third Annual Hawaii International Conference on Information Systems (Vol. 3), 336–345, 1991.

Goutas, S., Soupos, P., Christodoulakis, D., "Formalization of object-oriented database model with rules," *Information and Software Technology*, Vol. 33, Dec. 1991.

Gray, P., *Object-Oriented Databases: A Semantic Data Model Approach* (New York: Prentice-Hall, 1992).

Kersten, M., Schippers, F., "Towards an object-centered database language," International Workshop on Object-Oriented Database Systems, Proceedings, Wash., DC, IEEE Computer Society Press, 1986.

Kim, W., "Issues of Object-Oriented Database Schemas," doctoral thesis, University of Texas at Austin, 1988.

Kim, W., *Introduction to Object-Oriented Databases* (Cambridge, MA: The MIT Press, 1990).

Kim, W., "Research directions in object-oriented database systems," *Communications of the ACM*, 1990.

Liu, L., Horowitz, E., *Object Database Support for CASE* (Englewood Cliffs, NJ: Prentice-Hall, 1991).

Loomis, M., "Integrating objects with relational technology," *Object Magazine*, July/August 1991.

Loomis, M., "Object and relational technology. Can they cooperate?," *Object Magazine*, July/August 1991.

Loomis, M., Atwood, T., Cattel, R., Duhi, J., Ferran, G., Wade, D., "The ODMG object model," *Journal of Object-Oriented Programming*, June 1993.

Lyngbaek, P., Kent, W., "A data modeling methodology for the design and implementation of information systems," International Workshop on Object-Oriented Database Systems, Proceedings, Wash., DC, IEEE Computer Society Press, 1986.

Magedson, B., "Building OT from the bottom up," *Object Magazine*, July/August 1991.

Martin, J., Odell, J., *Object-Oriented Analysis and Design* (Englewood Cliffs, NJ: Prentice-Hall, 1992).

McFadden, F., "Conceptual design of object-oriented databases," *Journal of Object-Oriented Programming*, Vol. 4, Sept. 1991.

McFadden, F., Hoffer, J., *Database Management* (Menlo Park, CA: Benjamin Cummings Publishing Company, 1987).

Melton, J., "The MOOSE is loose," *Database Programming & Design,* May 1993.

Meyer, B., *Object-Oriented Software Construction* (Englewood Cliffs, NJ: Prentice Hall 1988).

Morgan, J., "Ingres for DB2 users," *Relational Database Journal*, May-July 1993.

Object Management Group, *Object Management Architecture Guide,* Second Edition (Framingham, MA: Object Management Group, 1992).

Object Management Group and Special Interest Group, *Object Analysis and Design* (Framingham, MA: Object Management Group, 1993).

Object Management Group and X/Open Co. Ltd., *The Common Object Request Broker: Architecture and Specification,* Revision 1.1 (Framingham, MA: Object Management Group, 1992).

Rentsch, B., "Object Oriented Programming Issues," Communications of the ACM, July 1982.

Rowe, L., "A shared object hierarchy," International Workshop on Object-Oriented Database Systems, Proceedings, Wash., DC, IEEE Computer Society Press, 1986.

Ruben, K., Goldberg, A., "Object behavior analysis," *Communications of the ACM*, September 1992.

Schek, H., Scholl, M., "Evolution of data models," International Workshop on Object-Oriented Database Systems, Proceedings, Wash., DC, IEEE Computer Society Press, 1990.

Scholl, M., Laasch, C., Tresch, M., "Updateable views in object-oriented databases," International Workshop on Object-Oriented Database Systems, Proceedings, Wash., DC, IEEE Computer Society Press, 1990.

Soloviev, V., "An overview of three commercial object-oriented database management systems: ONTOS, ObjectStore, and O/ sub 2/," *SIGMOD Record*, Vol. 21, March 1992.

Stone, C., "The rise of object databases: can the Object Management Group get database vendors to agree on object standards?," *DBMS*, July 1992.

Thalheim, B., "Extending the entity-relationship model for a high-level, theory-based database design," International Workshop on Object-Oriented Database Systems, Proceedings, Wash., DC, IEEE Computer Society Press, March 1990.

Unland, R., Schlageter, G., "Object-oriented database systems: concepts and perspectives," International Workshop on Object-Oriented Database Systems, Proceedings, Wash., DC, IEEE Computer Society Press, 1990.

Varma, S., "Object-oriented databases: where are we now?," *Database Programming & Design*, May 1993.

Vasan, R., "Relational databases and objects: a hybrid solution," *Object Magazine*, July/August 1991.

Yourdon, E., "The marriage of relational and object-oriented design," *Relational Journal*, Vol. 3, Issue 6, Jan. 1992.

Index